THE SAGA MONEY GUIDE

The
Saga Money Guide

Paul Lewis

UNWIN
PAPERBACKS

LONDON SYDNEY WELLINGTON

First published in Great Britain by Unwin Paperbacks,
an imprint of Unwin Hyman Limited, 1988.

Unwin Hyman Limited
15–17 Broadwick Street, London W1V 1FP

Allen & Unwin (Australia) Pty Ltd
8 Napier Street, North Sydney, NSW 2060, Australia

Allen & Unwin New Zealand Pty Ltd with the Port Nicholson Press
60 Cambridge Terrace, Wellington, New Zealand

British Library Cataloguing in Publication Data

Lewis, Paul
    Saga money guide. – (Saga Guides)
    1. Great Britain. Personal finance – For retired persons
    I. Title   II. Series
    332.024′0565
    ISBN 004 440175 2

Set in 12 on 13 point Plantin by Columns, Caversham, Reading
and printed in Great Britain by Cox & Wyman Ltd, Reading

CONTENTS

FOREWORD

Most people get money through work. When you retire and stop work, you are suddenly cut off from this source of funds. Instead, you will normally have at least a pension or some other social security benefit, perhaps some pension from your job, and possibly some income from investments. Even if you have never managed to save much, retirement age is the time when many people find they have redundancy payments or a lump sum from an insurance or pension policy.

How will you manage? What pension will you get? Will you be able to do some work? Will you have to pay tax? Where should your money be invested? How can you provide for your family? Where can you go for help? Should you make a will? Will your heirs have to pay tax when you die? These questions trouble most people when they think of retirement. However, as in the case of most financial questions, with a little information and some planning you can work out the answers.

This book will take some of the mystery out of these questions and provide answers to many of them.

THE SAGA MONEY GUIDE

1 RETIREMENT BUDGETING

There are three main sources of income for retired people – the state retirement pension, the pension from your job, and income from savings or from any capital you may get through redundancy or an insurance policy. How rich you feel – and how poor! – will depend on your share of these three things. It will also depend on how you manage your spending. This chapter looks at budgeting.

Managing Your Money

When you retire, your income will almost certainly go down, but so will many of your expenses. There will be no fares to work, no lunches or after-work drinks, no leaving presents to buy, and you will not have to dress the part. But these savings are not normally going to be enough to absorb all the loss of income. Some things, like heating, groceries, travel and hobbies, will cost you more. The impact of retirement will also depend on what perks you got at work. If you had a company car, free use of the firm's telephone and never had to buy a pen or notepad, you may find that life is suddenly very expensive. However, once you reach pension age you will get some concessions on the cost of travel and entertainment.

Because the changes are so many and pull in different directions, it is essential to write down the main things you spend your money on, how much they cost you now and what you think they will cost in retirement. Then you can see how much you can save – and afford – when you retire.

The list below is a guide to help you make such a list and gives brief advice about each item. More detailed information will be found both later in this book and in *Saga Rights Guide* in the same series, also by Paul Lewis.

Expenses

Home
Rates If your income is low after retirement, you may be able to get help with your rates through housing benefit.

Water and Sewerage Charges There are no concessions on grounds of age or income.

Rent or Mortgage If you pay rent and your income is low after retirement, you may be able to get help with your rent through housing benefit. If you still have a mortgage, you can only look forward to the day when it is paid off. Alternatively you could think of selling your home and buying somewhere cheaper or taking out a home income plan (see Chapter 4).

Electricity, Gas, Heating Costs You will probably use more electricity and gas when you retire because you will spend more time at home. If, before your retirement, no one was in during the working day, you will find that you are now using heating for as much as fifty hours more per week, and your bills could go up by 65% or more.

Insurance, Buildings and Contents Your insurance company may offer a discount on your contents insurance because you will be in the house more during the day.

Telephone You will probably find your telephone bill goes up, especially if you have been used to making personal calls from work. Try to avoid weekday daytime telephoning wherever possible, particularly during the peak period of 9am to 1pm.

Television (and Video) No rental companies seem to offer discounts to older people. But if you use a rented television and video more, you are getting better value for money! There are no general concessions on TV licences for older people.

Equipment – Service Contracts or HP If you get a lump-sum payment, it may be worthwhile paying off your HP commitments. But you may find that there are penalties in your contract for doing so.

Newsagent If you are used to reading a news-paper or magazine regularly, you should keep it up in retirement – don't lose touch! But you could consider going to the local library to read it if finances are tight.

Decoration and Repair Try not to economize too much. Delaying a repair can cost far more in the long run.

Food and Drink
Grocery Bills You will be eating at home more, and you may have more time to cook and save money by avoiding convenience foods. Retirement is a good time to consider your eating habits. Better ones may also be cheaper.

Pet Food Pets can be wonderful companions and some dogs can be useful protection. It's not a good idea to cut down on pets in retirement.

Alcoholic Drink for Home Many people find that the absence of work stresses means they drink less and save money.

Cigarettes and Tobacco Why not save money and prolong your life (and your partner's) by giving up?

Eating Out Yes, it's a luxury. But it's nice. Don't cut it out altogether: save it for those extra-special occasions.

Transport
Car Tax The burden of the cost of your car will depend on whether you have been lucky enough in the past to have had it paid by your employer. If retirement is your first experience of paying for your

motoring costs yourself, you are in for a shock. Car tax is £100 a year.

Car Insurance Shop around for insurance. You should consult an insurance broker. If you are in a motoring organization, they will probably act as a broker for you. Your age *can* help between fifty-five and seventy-five. After that, it can be a hindrance.

Car Maintenance You could turn an expense into a hobby. Consult your local council about adult education classes in car maintenance. More women are now taking it up.

Annual MOT Any car three years old or more needs an annual certificate of roadworthiness.

Motoring Organization Membership The security of a breakdown service is very important as you get older, especially if you intend to travel more. There are now alternatives to the AA and the RAC, but they do not offer the same range of financial and other services which you may find useful.

Petrol and Oil More than ever, it is worth shopping around. The well-known names are generally the dearest and petrol is just petrol. Petrol at motorway service stations is usually very expensive.

Bus Pass Most local councils offer some concessionary fares to people over sixty (men may have to wait until sixty-five). Many coach operators offer discounts.

Railcard Once you've retired you will probably want to travel more to see relatives and friends. A £15 railcard from British Rail, which lasts for a year, can save its cost on a single longer journey.

Bicycle Maintenance If you have more time now you're retired, pedalling there can save money and keep you fit. Keeping the bicycle well looked after will pay dividends.

Regular Fares Journeys to and from your nearest shopping centre may become more frequent.

Health and Wellbeing

Dentist The over-sixties have to pay dental charges just like anyone else. And from some time in 1988 even dental check-ups are going to cost money. The only help is on grounds of low income. But the expense should be a priority. Apart from all the other obvious benefits, keeping your own teeth helps keep you feeling young.

Optician and Glasses During 1988, the Government is planning to end free sight tests, though some opticians may still offer them. Regular sight tests are important as you get older. Not only is bad sight uncomfortable and dangerous; a sight test can reveal the onset of more serious eye problems in time to have them cured. People over sixty have to pay optician's charges just like anyone else. The only help is on grounds of low income.

Other Medical Treatment The NHS is free for the big things, though you may have to wait a long time for non-urgent treatment. However, some kinds of treatment, such as chiropody, physiotherapy, osteopathy, chiropractic, homeopathy or psychotherapy, normally have to be paid for. If you want this kind of treatment, ask your doctor if it is available on the NHS.

Chemists and Medicines If you are under pension age, prescriptions are very expensive. You may find that chemists will recommend a paid-for alternative to some items that is cheaper. Once you are pension age (sixty for a woman, sixty-five for a man), prescriptions are free (except for some things such as elastic stockings). Remember that chemists make a lot of their profit from vitamin supplements and nonessential 'health' items. Just because a chemist sells something does not mean that it is necessarily good for *you*.

Cosmetics and Hairdresser If you are used to spending money on cosmetics or hairdressing, remember that looking and feeling good are even more important for your self-confidence as you get older. Many hairdressers offer free or cheap hairdressing to the over-sixties.

Vet Bills If your pet needs a lot of veterinary care, consider taking out an addition to your house contents insurance policy. It may work out cheaper.

Clothes

Regular Purchase Once you stop work, you are freed from the obligation to look the part at your job. Not only will that save you money, but it may also provide you with an opportunity to think about what style you want to adopt in retirement.

Clubs or Credit Cards Rolling credit cards attached to a shop or chain of shops can be a very expensive form of credit. Normally you pay a fixed amount each month and are allowed to spend (that is borrow!) up to thirty times your monthly payment. Clubs where someone calls to collect a regular sum off you each week are similar, but interest rates can be even higher. Try to use an ordinary credit card (Visa or Access) or a bank loan if you cannot pay directly.

Cleaning and Repair You should spend less servicing your clothes when you retire.

Recreation

Cinema, Theatre Many cinemas and theatres offer cheaper tickets to people over sixty. And afternoon shows are often cheaper, especially during the week.

Books, Magazines, Records, CDs, Tapes, Videos

If you've been in the habit of buying these, remember that your local library now probably lets you borrow them all (except videos) for nothing.

Clubs and Hobbies   A new hobby can be one of the pleasures of retirement and it can lead to new friends.

Pub   Still the centre of many people's social life, but you may be surprised at how much it costs you if you work it out.

Pools or Other Gambling   Some people cannot resist the chance of getting something for nothing, even when they know it will probably cost them money in the long run. If you enjoy gambling, look on it as a hobby and work out the real cost.

Evening Classes   Adult education classes are held as often in the day as the evening nowadays. Many people find retirement a wonderful chance to catch up on the interests or study they missed during a busy working life. These classes are usually inexpensive.

Sports   Keeping fit is more important as we get older. Most sports centres offer reduced membership and entry to people over sixty. Modern swimming baths are kept very warm and you can get a cheap half-day of exercise in a warm environment. Alternatively, free exercise classes are often provided by local Age Concern groups.

Gardening   Probably the most popular hobby in retirement. You will be tempted to spend more once you stop work.

Holidays   There has never been a better choice of holidays for older people. Apart from the well-known specialist company Saga Holidays (address in the Appendix to this book), other companies now have special deals for people over fifty-five. Remember that if you take a longer holiday during the winter you will save money on heating, winter clothes and other items.

Finance

Life Assurance Your life assurance will probably end when you reach pension age, as will contributions to your pension scheme. Remember that if you go on working up to pension age (sixty for a woman, sixty-five for a man), you should pay no National Insurance contributions on any payday *after* you reach that age.

Regular Investments and Savings When you retire you should re-appraise your whole approach to saving, investment and finance.

Bank Charges Special concessions by banks for people over sixty generally have ended. All the main banks now offer free banking to everyone who keeps in credit. It's worth studying the rules to make sure that you keep inside the free banking limit. Some banks offer a special package for people over fifty-five, including free financial advice and reductions on the cost of services.

Interest on Loans and Credit Charges Do try to avoid taking on any new commitments. And avoid like the plague any loans to clear debts which use your home as collateral.

Miscellaneous and Personal

Stationery and Postage Items that seemed to cost a fairly insignificant amount when you had a job may now seem to swallow up a noticeable chunk of your income.

Christmas or Birthday Presents.

Donations to Charity Surprisingly, it is the people who have the least money who give the most to charity.

Payments to Relatives Even when you retire, there may still be older or younger relatives for whom you take some financial responsibility.

Pocket Money It is important that you do have some allowance for the things you don't want to tell anyone about.

Cutting it Down

When you have done your 'before' and 'after' expenses list, go through it deciding what is really necessary and what is not. Remember that hobbies and care of yourself are not luxuries. Doing without everything except food, drink and warmth is not a sensible way to economize unless you are absolutely forced to do so. If you live alone, it is especially important to provide for the cost of activities which help you meet people. And if you have a partner, there must be even more fairness and openness between you when your income is lower.

Income

It is useful to do a 'before' and 'after' calculation for your income as well as your expenditure. The income list always looks a lot shorter than the expenditure list. But there may well be new opportunities to earn or make extra money.

Wages or Salary Remember to use the net figure. You may find you keep much more of modest earnings after retirement than higher earnings before (see Chapters 5 and 6).

Part-time Work Make sure that you do not lose your pension or social security benefits and that you pay no National Insurance (see Chapter 3).

Investments If you have money to invest, make sure that some of it is invested where tax is not deducted at source and some where you can get at it quickly (see Chapter 7).

Pension from Your Job(s)   Try to find out how your pension from your job will change, if at all, over the years. And make sure that you chase up all the pensions you may have earned during your working life (see Chapter 2).

State Pension(s)   You will lose some or all of your state pension if you earn more than £75 a week (see Chapter 3).

Other Social Security Benefits   Many social security benefits come with restrictions on earning or travelling abroad.

Any Other Income   There are many opportunities to turn your time and talents to income once you are retired (see Chapter 2).

Gifts from Relatives   You may have relatives who are in a position regularly to assist you financially once you retire.

Your Home   You may consider a home income plan (see Chapter 4) or even letting a room.

Comparison

Once you have written down estimates, all expenses and all income, you will begin to see how you will manage in retirement. Try to see just how much you will have to cut down to live within your means. This simple exercise will take a lot of the fear out of the prospect of retirement.

2 EARNINGS RELATED PENSIONS

Most people retiring today have a pension related to their earnings in addition to their basic state pension. This pension can come from two sources – the state earnings related pension scheme (nowadays called SERPS) and/or a pension from your employer. If you have had several employers, it is possible that you have an entitlement to several separate pensions. In other cases your contributions will have been transferred with you from job to job.

Since April 1978 almost everyone at work has had to pay into an extra pension scheme on top of the basic state pension. The exceptions are as follows:

- People under sixteen or over pension age pay no National Insurance contributions at all.
- People who earn less than a certain amount pay no National Insurance contributions at all. This limit is called the lower earnings limit and is currently £41 a week.
- Married women and widows who pay the lower married woman's contribution make no payment at all towards a pension.
- Self-employed people contribute only to the basic state pension, although their contributions are partly related to their earnings.

Everyone else must pay either into the state earnings related pension scheme (SERPS) or into a scheme which gives a pension which is at least as good. People who pay into one of these private schemes are described as contracted out of the state scheme and pay a slightly lower rate of National Insurance contributions than other employees. Some people pay into a private scheme as well as paying into the state scheme; they pay the full rate of National Insurance contributions.

The State Earnings Related Pension Scheme

Since 1978 National Insurance contributions have been related to earnings. Currently, an employee pays 9% of his or her earnings up to a ceiling called the upper earnings limit. Currently that limit is £305 a week. No contributions are paid by the employee on earnings above that amount. In return for these contributions the Government undertakes to pay a pension related to earnings when the employee reaches pension age and retires.

The way this pension is calculated is fairly complicated. First, average earnings have more than doubled between 1978 and 1987. So the Government has to 'revalue' each year's earnings to take account of the increase. Second, the pension is not related to all your earnings. It is just related to the earnings between the lower earnings limit and the upper earnings limit. No contributions are paid above the upper earnings limit and the contributions paid on earnings below the lower earnings limit are just for your basic pension.

When these two adjustments have been made, your

revalued earnings for each year are added together and you get $\frac{1}{80}$ of the total as your annual additional pension. That is then divided by 52 to give the weekly amount.

Because the additional pension is earnings related, non-manual workers generally receive more than manual workers and men generally receive more than women simply because their pay is higher. A man retiring in 1988/89 with average manual worker's pay and absences since 1978 will get £19.95 a week additional pension. A woman with the same work history will get £10.01. The maximum additional pension paid to someone retiring in 1988/89 is £34 a week. But to receive that you would have had to earn one and a half times the average manual male wage or twice the average non-manual female wage consistently for all those ten years.

Working It Out
To work out your own additional pension you will need to know what you earned in each tax year from 1978/79 to 1987/88. For each tax year starting with 1978/79, you take the earnings on which you paid full National Insurance contributions. If those earnings are more than the upper earnings limit for the year, you use that limit instead. You increase those earnings by a factor to take account of the rise in earnings generally. You then subtract the annual amount of the 1987/88 lower earnings limit, which is £2,028. The result is your 'surplus' for that year. If the result is less than zero, you call it zero. You add all these surpluses up and divide by 80 to get your annual additional pension and by 52 to get your weekly pension. If you have a calculator you can just divide once by 4,160.

The easiest way to do the calculation is to set it out

in a table. Tables 1, 2 (on pages 16 and 17) and 3 (on page 18) show how John, an average manual worker, Mary, an average non-manual worker, and Matthew, a higher-paid man, filled in the table.

John worked for the Post Office for the whole period from 1978/79 until his retirement in July 1988. He had some old records of his pay and a friend in the Post Office wages department looked up the rest. His earnings were always below the upper earnings limit so he used his actual earnings to work out his surplus. When he added up the surpluses and divided by 4,160, he found that his pension came out to £19.95 a week, just about what the DHSS offered him.

Mary was a secretary/administrator on an average sort of wage for a woman. She was made redundant in 1982/83 and took some time to get another job. She did not pay enough contributions to have any surplus in that year, so she put down zero as the surplus for that year. But her final pension was fairly typical for an average-paid woman. Being a meticulous sort of person, Mary had all her records.

Matthew was a manager with an office equipment company. He was paid above the upper earnings limit until his firm went bust in 1981/82. He took a few weeks to get another job and the pay was lower. So for that year and for the next two years he earned less than the upper earnings limit. However, after that, promotion and increments ensured his earnings were above the upper earnings limit for the last four years before retirement. Matthew had filled in a tax return every year, so he could look up his earnings from his own tax file.

Now you should be able to fill in the blank Table 4 (on page 19) with your earnings and calculate your own additional pension.

Table 1

John's Additional Pension Calculation (£)

Year	Upper earnings limit	John's earnings	Revaluation factor	Earnings × revaluation factor	1986/87 lower earnings limit	Surplus
1978/79	6,240	4,244 ×	2.586 =	10,975 −	2,028 =	8,947
1979/80	7,020	4,909 ×	2.281 =	11,197 −	2,028 =	9,169
1980/81	8,580	5,782 ×	1.906 =	11,020 −	2,028 =	8,992
1981/82	10,400	6,204 ×	1.596 =	9,902 −	2,028 =	7,874
1982/83	11,440	6,989 ×	1.450 =	10,134 −	2,028 =	8,106
1983/84	12,220	7,426 ×	1.347 =	10,003 −	2,028 =	7,975
1984/85	13,000	7,987 ×	1.247 =	9,960 −	2,028 =	7,932
1985/86	13,780	8,710 ×	1.170 =	10,191 −	2,028 =	8,163
1986/87	14,820	9,277 ×	1.074 =	9,963 −	2,028 =	7,935
1987/88	15,340	9,926 ×	1.000 =	9,926 −	2,028 =	7,898
					Total surplus =	82,991

Weekly additional pension = 82,991 divided by 4,160 = £19.95

Table 2
Mary's Additional Pension Calculation (£)

Year	Upper earnings limit	John's earnings		Revaluation factor		Earnings × revaluation factor		1986/87 lower earnings limit		Surplus
1978/79	6,240	2,927	×	2.586	=	7,569	−	2,028	=	5,541
1979/80	7,020	3,386	×	2.281	=	7,723	−	2,028	=	5,695
1980/81	8,580	3,988	×	1.906	=	7,601	−	2,028	=	5,573
1981/82	10,400	4,493	×	1.596	=	7,171	−	2,028	=	5,143
1982/83	11,440	1,200	×	1.450	=	1,740	−	2,028	=	0
1983/84	12,220	5,522	×	1.347	=	7,438	−	2,028	=	5,410
1984/85	13,000	6,022	×	1.247	=	7,509	−	2,028	=	5,481
1985/86	13,780	6,526	×	1.170	=	7,635	−	2,028	=	5,607
1986/87	14,820	7,062	×	1.074	=	7,585	−	2,028	=	5,557
1987/88	15,340	7,556	×	1.000	=	7,556	−	2,028	=	5,528
							Total surplus		=	49,535

Weekly additional pension = 49,535 divided by 4,160 = £11.91

Table 3
Matthew's Additional Pension Calculation (£)

Year	Upper earnings limit	John's earnings		Revaluation factor		Earnings × revaluation factor		1986/87 lower earnings limit		Surplus
1978/79	**6,240**	6,500	×	2.586	=	16,137	−	2,028	=	14,109
1979/80	**7,020**	7,200	×	2.281	=	16,013	−	2,028	=	13,985
1980/81	**8,580**	9,000	×	1.906	=	16,353	−	2,028	=	14,325
1981/82	10,400	**7,600**	×	1.596	=	12,130	−	2,028	=	10,102
1982/83	11,440	**10,500**	×	1.450	=	15,225	−	2,028	=	13,197
1983/84	12,220	**12,000**	×	1.347	=	16,164	−	2,028	=	14,136
1984/85	**13,000**	13,100	×	1.247	=	16,211	−	2,028	=	14,183
1985/86	**13,780**	14,500	×	1.170	=	16,123	−	2,028	=	14,095
1986/87	**14,820**	16,000	×	1.074	=	15,917	−	2,028	=	13,889
1987/88	**15,340**	17,500	×	1.000	=	15,340	−	2,028	=	13,312
								Total surplus	=	135,333

Weekly additional pension = 135,333 divided by 4,160 = £32.53

Bold figures are the ones Matthew used – the lower of the two figures. In 1981/82 the table exaggerates his earnings by £150 and his surplus by £240 and his final pension by 6p a week. See Note 2 below.

18

Table 4

Your Additional Pension Calculation (£)

Year	Upper earnings limit	John's earnings		Revaluation factor		Earnings × revaluation factor	1986/87 lower earnings limit	Your Surplus
1978/79	6,240		×	2.586	=		− 2,028 =	
1979/80	7,020		×	2.281	=		− 2,028 =	
1980/81	8,580		×	1.906	=		− 2,028 =	
1981/82	10,400		×	1.596	=		− 2,028 =	
1982/83	11,440		×	1.450	=		− 2,028 =	
1983/84	12,220		×	1.347	=		− 2,028 =	
1984/85	13,000		×	1.247	=		− 2,028 =	
1985/86	13,780		×	1.170	=		− 2,028 =	
1986/87	14,820		×	1.074	=		− 2,028 =	
1987/88	15,340		×	1.000	=		− 2,028 =	

Total surplus =

Weekly additional pension = total surplus divided by 4,160 =

Notes

1 These tables apply only to people who reach pension age between 6 April 1988 and 5 April 1989. Older people will have smaller additional pensions.

2 People who earn above the upper earnings limit for part of a tax year but whose total earnings in the year are below the limit will find that the table exaggerates their surplus for that year.

find that the table exaggerates their surplus for that year.

19

What You Earned

If you have not kept records of your earnings (your employer should give you a form called a P60 every year setting them out for that year), there are three sources from which you can try to obtain them.

First, your employer may well hold records and be willing to give you the figures. However, many employers do not keep records for more than seven years and if they have gone out of business there may be problems even with more recent information. And, of course, they do not have to help if they decide it is too much trouble.

Second, your tax office should have the information. However, if you have changed jobs, they may have to contact other tax offices for the older material. It would help if you sent them details of all your employers during the period. The tax authorities are obliged to keep records for only seven years, although they often do keep them for longer. The more places they have to contact, the longer it is going to take you to get the information from them. But eventually they should let you have the details, as long as they still have them.

Third, you might expect the Department of Health and Social Security (DHSS) to hold the information. Surprisingly, they do not. For years before 1987/88 they hold information on the contributions you have paid but not on the earnings on which they were based. They will be reluctant to do the calculations of earnings for you. However, if all else fails, you should write to them. The information is held at the DHSS Headquarters in Newcastle, but you must ask your local DHSS office to get the information from Newcastle for you.

As an alternative to finding the information, you can use an approximation. If you have had much the same sort of job for the last ten years, you can just use last year's earnings and multiply them by ten to give your total surplus. Divide that figure by 80 and then 52 (or by 4,160) to give your approximate weekly additional pension.

Older and Younger
The examples and tables will give the right answer only for people who reach pension age between 6 April 1988 and 5 April 1989. Older people will generally get lower additional pensions. The maximum additional pension currently paid to anyone retiring in the years from 1979/80 to date is shown in Table 5 below.

Younger people can do the calculation to give them an idea of the additional pension they have already earned. But they can also now obtain an official forecast of their pension from the DHSS. You should get form BR.19 from your local DHSS office and send it off.

If you are not contracted out of the state scheme,

Table 5

	Maximum additional pension	
Retirement year	*At retirement (£)*	*Now (£)*
1979/80	1.28	2.70
1980/81	2.90	5.12
1981/82	5.25	7.96
1982/83	8.46	11.75
1983/84	11.70	14.65
1984/85	15.08	18.22
1985/86	19.07	21.92
1986/87	23.26	24.99
1987/88	28.49	29.68
1988/89	34.00	34.00

the additional pension is paid to you with your basic retirement pension. If you are contracted out of the state scheme and pay into a private scheme, that scheme must guarantee to give you a pension of at least as much as the additional pension when you retire. This pension they must guarantee is called your guaranteed minimum pension or GMP. (In fact the GMP is calculated slightly differently from the additional pension. Normally it is exactly the same, but there are circumstances in which it may be slightly more or slightly less.) Your actual pension from your scheme may be more than this GMP when you retire.

When You Retire
Unlike most company pensions, the additional pension from the state is fully protected against inflation once it has been awarded. It goes up each April along with the basic retirement pension. However, your company pension may well not go up with inflation. And the GMP remains fixed at the amount calculated when you retire. Each year the DHSS calculates the additional pension you would have received had you remained within the SERPS. If that additional pension is more than the GMP (not the pension you actually get), the DHSS pays the difference as an addition to your basic retirement pension. It is called payable additional pension. As time passes, most people find that they get some payable additional pension as well as their company pension.

Many people have been confused by receiving a letter from the DHSS setting out their pension entitlement with the phrase 'guaranteed minimum pension' and a figure by it. Naturally enough they have assumed that they would get that amount as a pension. In fact, they do not. It just lets you know the minimum pension you should get from your company scheme, and that if you do not the DHSS will make it up.

The system is slightly different for people who receive a pension from the civil service or a local authority or any other public service paying authority such as a nationalized industry. But the result is the same.

Other Matters

If you do not retire and draw your pension at sixty or sixty-five, your additional pension will be increased by 1% for each seven weeks you delay. However, it will not be increased if you are drawing any other social security benefit such as invalidity pension or widow's benefit instead of drawing retirement pension.

A widow or widower normally inherits the additional pension from their late husband or wife. But there is a limit to how much can be inherited if the widow or widower has their own additional pension as well. In that case the total additional pension paid cannot be more than someone of the same age could have earned on maximum earnings since April 1978. So no one can have an additional pension bigger than those set out in Table 5 on page 21.

You can be paid an additional pension on your full contributions from 1978/79 even if you have not paid enough full contributions to get a basic pension.

There are more details about the basic state pension in *Saga Rights Guide*, also by Paul Lewis in this series.

Company Pensions

About half of all the people at work belong to a company pension scheme of some sort. In the public sector these schemes are often called superannuation. All schemes work on the same basic principle. During your working life, you and your employer pay into a fund. When you retire, that fund pays you benefits. But the details of what you pay and what you receive differ widely from one scheme to another.

What You Pay In

In most schemes you and your employer pay in a fixed percentage of your earnings. The amount you pay in can vary from nothing up to 15%. Above 15% you get no tax relief on your contributions, so they become less attractive. Your employer usually contributes as much as or more than you, sometimes very much more. In some schemes, notably the civil service scheme, the employer pays the whole cost; you pay nothing.

When you approach retirement, you can usually pay extra contributions from your final years' salaries. These extra amounts are called additional voluntary contributions. As long as you do not exceed the limit of 15% of total earnings, you get full tax relief on these contributions and they can boost your final pension considerably. There is a slightly higher limit for the self-employed.

What You Get Out

The better schemes offer you a pension which is a proportion of your final salary. Normally, they pay you one eightieth or one sixtieth of your final salary for each year you have been in the scheme. So after forty years' service you will get a half (forty eightieths) or two thirds (forty sixtieths) of your final year's earnings. As some people find that their earnings go down in the year or so before retiring, some schemes allow you to choose the best of your final few years.

The pension you receive on retirement may well be fixed at that level forever. Alternatively, it may be increased in line with inflation or by a fixed annual percentage, usually 3% or 5%. Civil service pensions and those paid to all other public servants, such as NHS workers, teachers, firemen, local authority workers and those employed by nationalized industries, all go up in line with inflation. In the private sector such generosity is rare. Indeed, not many pension funds could afford it.

For people who remain in one pension scheme all their working life, these final salary schemes can provide very good pensions. But if you leave your job before retirement age, you are not treated so well. In the past you could simply lose all your pension rights. You were given back your contributions, less a deduction for income tax. But you did not get back the contributions paid by your employer. They were kept in the scheme and helped pay the benefits of those who remained until retirement age. The pensions paid to many people are actually partly funded by the losses of early leavers.

If you left more recently, and have worked in the scheme for at least five years (two years from 6 April 1988), you are likely to find that your pension has been 'frozen'. That means that the contributions of you and your employer remain in the scheme and you remain entitled at retirement to a proportion of your last earnings in the last year before you left the scheme. Normally those earnings will seem very low today and a few 60ths or 80ths of them will be a pretty paltry pension.

Since 1978 anyone who was in a contracted-out pension must have their pension 'preserved' rather than frozen. It is still related to your earnings in the last year before you left the scheme. But the pension to which you are entitled must be increased each year in line with the increase in earnings generally.

Other Schemes

Some schemes relate the pension to your average salary over all your working life or pay you a certain amount for each year's service. But these are rare.

More common are the so-called 'money-purchase' schemes which save up the contributions paid by you and your employer. These contributions are invested, usually in the stock market, and when you reach pension age the accumulated fund is used to buy you a pension. These schemes cannot make any guarantees about the amount of the final fund or the amount of the pension it will buy. They can be better or worse than final-salary schemes. But they are much more uncertain. These schemes are not generally contracted out of the state scheme and are quite common as schemes which top up the SERPS and among self-employed people.

Lump Sums

Many schemes provide an opportunity for you to get a tax-free lump sum out of your scheme on retirement. Some give it to you automatically; in others you can forfeit some of your pension to get a lump sum. A lump sum of up to one and a half times your final year's earnings is tax-free. There are no general rules about whether it is worth giving up part of your pension in order to get a lump sum. You should take account of the fact that the pension is taxable, whereas the lump sum is taxfree. But remember that the price of a lump sum is a reduction in your pension which will make you worse off each month until you die.

Many people have used additional voluntary contributions as a way of boosting their lump sum rather than their pension. That is no longer possible for new schemes. But if you are already in a scheme it is a very worthwhile way of bypassing the tax on earnings in your last few years of work.

Early and Late Retirement
Many schemes specify different retirement ages for men and women. It is still legal for schemes to do so, although it is not now lawful for an employer to specify different retirement ages for men and women. Most schemes allow early retirement, though you will get reduced benefits as you will be drawing a pension for longer. Schemes also allow you to defer your retirement. Schemes that are contracted out of the SERPS must revalue your pension by 7½% a year for each year you delay. Other schemes will have different arrangements.

Checking Your Company Pension
Before you leave your job it is as well to check how much your pension is going to be and that you are happy with the calculation. You have a right to a document (usually obtained from your employer) setting out how the scheme works and how your pension is worked out. If you belong to a union, it can often help you deal with any queries. In particular the civil service and local government unions are very good at dealing with pension problems.

If you have changed jobs, it is as well to check up on any rights you may have from the pension scheme of any job you have left. It is up to you to inform the people who administer the scheme if you change your address. If you can get no information from your previous employer or through your union, the DHSS may be able to help.

Changes

Over the last few years the Government has introduced a lot of major changes in company and private pensions. Many are happening in 1988. Most of them affect only people who are not yet retired. And they will be of real interest only to younger people and the self-employed.

From 1 July 1988 people in SERPS or a company scheme which is opted out of SERPS will be able to leave and join their own private pension plan instead. The DHSS will pay into the scheme the earnings related contributions that would have gone to the SERPS or their company scheme. And they will get a 2% bonus paid in as well until April 1993. This option is not likely to be attractive to people in good final-salary schemes or to older people.

Effect on Social Security Benefits

Nowadays a pension from your job may affect your right to social security benefits. There are two ways it can do so.

Some social security benefits depend on your income. The main ones are income support, housing benefit (help with rates and rent), help with optical or dental charges, and legal aid. Any pension you have will increase your income and reduce your chances of help from these sources.

However, a pension from a job can also affect some other social security benefits directly.

Men and women aged between fifty-five and pension age who claim unemployment benefit will find it is reduced if they receive a pension from their job of more than £35 a week. For each 10p above £35 their benefit will be reduced by 10p. So a single person's unemployment benefit of £32.75 will disappear as the pension reaches £67.80 a week. A married man will lose all his benefit of £52.95 if his pension is £88 or more. And he will lose £20.20 of it if his wife has earnings or a pension from her job of £20.20 or more.

A man who receives an addition to his retirement pension for his wife where she is under sixty will lose that addition if her income from earnings or a pension from her job exceeds £32.75. A man who receives an addition to his retirement pension for a dependent child will lose that addition if his wife has an income from earnings or a pension from her job of £90 or more. The law which introduced the rule that allowed a woman's pension from her job to be counted in the same way as her earnings was introduced in November 1984. However, it was found to be faulty and anyone who suffered a deduction under it may be entitled to a refund. A new law was passed in 1988 to correct the law and enable the Government to count the pension from a job of a married woman in the same way as earnings. But if you had an addition for a wife deducted because of their pension from their job prior to April 1988, you should write to your local social security office and ask them to check that you were correctly treated. You may well get a refund.

3 WORKING IN RETIREMENT

People retire younger and fitter today than they used to. Most people enjoy their leisure and new freedom from the pressure of work. But many also feel that they still have something to offer and would be glad to earn a little money for giving it. This chapter looks at the opportunities and problems in part-time or volunteer work.

Working Before Pension Age

If you retire from your job before the state pension age of sixty for a woman or sixty-five for a man, you may be able to claim unemployment benefit or, if you retired on grounds of ill health, sickness benefit or invalidity pension. If your income is very low you may be able to claim income support which is paid at a higher level once you reach sixty, although the amount is still low. Each of these benefits carries strict rules about working.

Unemployment Benefit If you claim unemployment benefit, you must be available for work. Every time you sign on at the unemployment benefit office you declare that you are not working. Accepting any job will normally end your right to benefit. However, you can work provided that you do not earn more than £2 a day and you are still available for work. If you do not earn a specific amount per day, the DHSS will normally average the amount you get over the days you work. In some cases where you are working for a charity offering a service to the community, you do not have to be available immediately, but usually within twenty-four hours.

Unemployment benefit is paid for each day of unemployment from Monday to Saturday. So working on one day will end that day's benefit. Days are assessed from midnight to midnight so evening work counts and night work may affect two days' benefit. However, paid work on a Sunday does not count at all. Part-time work may only affect your benefit on the days you work. However, if part-time work used to be your normal working pattern, you will not be allowed to claim benefit on the other days. And if the part-time work reduces your chance of getting a full-time job, you will not get benefit for the other days.

Unemployment benefit is taxable.

Sickness Benefit and Invalidity Pension are paid on the basis that you are incapable of work because of illness. However, it is possible that you can be allowed to work for therapeutic reasons. If you need to do that, your doctor and the DHSS have to agree beforehand. The work normally has to be very different from any sort of formal employment and must fit in around your illness. You cannot earn more than £27 a week from therapeutic work. If your earnings vary, they must not generally be above £27.

If you have an adult dependant such as a husband or wife, you will get extra sickness benefit or invalidity pension for him or her. That will be stopped if the dependant has earnings (including any pension from their job) of more than £19.40 for sickness benefit or £32.75 for invalidity pension.

Sickness benefit and invalidity pension are not taxable.

Income Support or Housing Benefit If you claim income support or receive housing benefit, your earnings count as income and reduce your benefit. The first £5 a week of earnings (£5 each for a couple) are ignored (and in some cases it can be up to £15), but anything above that reduces your income support penny for penny and your housing benefit at the rate of 6½p a week off your rent rebate and 2p a week off your rates rebate for every 10p a week earned.

Income support paid to someone under pension age is taxable. Housing benefit is not taxable.

Calculating Earnings
Earnings are net earnings after deducting tax and National Insurance. Except for income support and housing benefit, you can also deduct any expenses of working including travel, 15p towards a meal, and anything else which is reasonable and incurred because of the work. If you work occasionally or irregularly, your earnings are counted for the period to which they relate. For example, if you do one day's work and get one day's pay, you cannot average the amount out over a longer period.

National Insurance
Everyone under pension age has to pay National Insurance contributions if their earnings exceed £41 a week (this amount changes in April each year).

The contributions are normally 9% of earnings up to £305 a week. But since October 1985 people on low incomes have paid lower contributions. The current rates are 9% of all your earnings up to £305 a week if you earn £105 or more; 7% on all your earnings if you earn between £70 and £105 a week; and 5% on all your earnings if you earn between £41 and £70 a week. If you pay into a company pension scheme or, after 1 July 1988, an approved personal pension plan, your contributions will be 2% lower in each case. If you earn below £41 a week you do not pay contributions at all.

If you work after reaching pension age, you should not pay any National Insurance contributions. Your liability to pay contributions stops on the last payday *before* you reach that age. You should ask your employer to check that you are not paying contributions for any payday after your sixtieth or sixty-fifth birthday.

The employer now has to pay contributions for all adult employees earning over £41 week, including those over pension age and married women. However, there are lower rates for employees who earn less than £155 a week, but the employer now pays contributions on earnings above the ceiling of £305 as well.

Working After Pension Age

Retiring
When you reach pension age (sixty for a woman and sixty-five for a man), you cannot simply claim your pension. First, you must retire. That normally means that you must earn less than £75 a week, or work fewer than twelve hours a week, or work only occasionally. However, the DHSS may regard you as retired if your work is what they call 'not inconsistent with retirement'. These rules about retiring apply for only five years after pension age, until you reach sixty-five if you are a woman or seventy if you are a

man. After that you can claim your pension whatever you do.

A married woman who has no entitlement to a pension on her own contributions cannot get her married woman's pension on her husband's contributions until he retires and claims his pension. This rule applies whatever her age. So a woman married to a younger man can face a very long wait for a pension.

Earnings Rules

Even if you do retire, you are not free to earn whatever you like in those first five years after pension age. If you earn over a certain amount, the Government takes back some of your pension under the earnings rule. In fact, there are now several earnings rules.

Under the basic earnings rule, your pension will be reduced if you earn more than £75 a week. You lose 5p of your pension for every 10p of your first £4 earnings over the limit. And you lose 5p pension for every 5p earned over this amount. The current basic single pension will vanish completely as earnings reach £118.15.

A married man will lose all his own basic pension at the same level. His wife will lose her pension on his contributions as her earnings reach £101.75. Her pension cannot be lost by her husband's earnings. A man with a dependent wife under sixty can lose all his pension, including the extra paid for her, through his own earnings if they reach £142.90. The pension paid for her is also affected by her earnings (see below).

Fees and Occasional Work

If you are paid each week as an employee, the earnings rule calculation is straightforward. But if you work occasionally, there are special rules about how your earnings are counted.

If you simply work occasionally or irregularly as an employee or on a 'casual' basis, your earnings are counted for the period to which they relate. For example if you do one week's work and get one week's pay of £120, that would wipe out one week's pension. In either case, your earnings are net earnings after deducting tax and National Insurance and any expenses of working including travel, 15p towards a meal, and anything else which is reasonable and incurred because of the work.

However, there are special rules for people over retirement age (and their dependants) who are self-employed. It is generally a great advantage to be counted as self-employed (see Chapter 5 for the tax implications).

If you are self-employed, you do not take off the various expenses listed earlier. Instead you are assessed on your taxable profit as set out in your tax return. That profit is averaged out over the year. That means that you can have an annual taxable profit of £3,900 before the earnings rule begins to affect you, even if you receive fees in any one week which are considerably more than £75.

The DHSS will assess your pension on the expected profit for the year and reduce your pension accordingly. You will be expected to submit your tax accounts to them once the Inland Revenue have approved them. If the expected figure turns out to be wrong, they will then adjust your current pension accordingly.

Lodgers

If you have income from a boarder, you can be treated as self-employed if you are taxed in that way.

Alternatively, your 'profit' from the boarder is assessed by subtracting £6 from the payment he or she makes and then dividing by two. If you do not provide the lodger with full board, the £6 can be reduced by the DHSS, perhaps even to nothing so that your 'profit' would just be half the amount they pay.

Earnings Rules for Dependants

The earnings rules that apply to money paid for dependants are now harsher than those that apply to the basic pension.

A woman aged less than sixty is in a complicated position. There are two different earnings rules which may apply, depending on when her husband first received extra benefit for her. If he received it before 16 September 1985, she can earn up to £45 a week before he loses any of the extra paid for her. If her earnings exceed £45, the extra pension is reduced by 5p for every 10p earned up to £4 extra and by 5p for each 5p over that. So the extra £24.75 vanishes as her earnings reach £71.75.

However, if her husband first received the extra pension for her after 15 September 1985, there is an even stricter rule. The additional pension paid for her will disappear at once if her earnings exceed £32.75. Moreover, 'earnings' in this case include any pension paid from her job. Strictly speaking, prior to April 1988 this rule applied only where the woman had a pension from her job *and* earnings. Many women had their pension stopped wrongly. If you think that you may have been one of them, call into your DHSS office and ask for your case to be reviewed.

Other Points

The earnings rule is used to reduce only your basic pension. There is no reduction of your graduated pension or the additional pension related to your earnings after 5 April 1978. But any extra you earned on your basic pension by working past pension age can be reduced or lost completely if your earnings are high enough. The reduction of your basic pension by the earnings rule is quite separate from tax.

There is no reduction of a widow's pension whatever her earnings, though if she is over sixty and claiming a retirement pension she may lose a small amount of that. A widow who has remarried and earns over £75 a week may lose some of her retirement pension paid on her late husband's contributions.

If you work after reaching pension age, you should not pay any National Insurance contributions. Your liability to pay contributions stops on the last payday *before* you reach that age. You should ask your employer to check that you are not paying contributions.

Married Women

Some married women still retain the right to pay a lower rate of contribution, 3.85% of their earnings. If you still work, you should ask the local DHSS office for advice as to whether it would be worth your while to revoke your right. Ask them if you would have any right to a pension of your own at the age of sixty or could obtain a pension by paying some back contributions. Make sure that you get their advice in writing in case it turns out they advise you wrongly. If you want to revoke your right to pay lower contributions, obtain leaflet NI.1 from your local DHSS office and fill in the form, CF.9, at the back of it.

Self-employed

Many people who retire and work will do so only occasionally, either as a consultant for a fee or informally for cash. All this income is potentially taxable and should be declared to the Inland Revenue. Companies have to inform the Inland Revenue of the fees they pay and the people to whom they pay them.

If you intend to do such work regularly, it is well worth becoming self-employed. You will then be able to offset many expenses against the income and, depending on when you choose the date of your financial year, you can pay your tax up to two years in arrears. There are more details about tax in Chapters 5 and 6.

If you want to work but do not know quite what to do, you should ask yourself what you want to get out of work. If it is principally company, a sense of usefulness, or to combat a fear of stagnating at home rather than the financial reward, you could consider voluntary work. However, be aware that voluntary work often means more than not being paid. You may find that you are not only working for nothing, but also paying for petrol, stationery and telephone calls. Voluntary work of that sort is more like a hobby than a cost-free way of contributing to society.

Your local Age Concern or Citizens Advice Bureau may well know of opportunities, both paid and voluntary, for older people locally. They are both in the phone book (see the Appendix on page 110 for national addresses).

The Pre-Retirement Association, 19 Undine Street, London SW17 8PP (tel: 01–767 3225), publishes a free leaflet, *Work In Retirement*, which lists organizations and agencies that will help you find work. And the *Yearbook of Recruitment and Employment Services*, from the Federation of Employment and Recruitment Services, should be in your local library.

If you want to do voluntary work, you could get in touch with your local Council of Voluntary Service (or Volunteer Bureau) – find this in the phone book under 'V'; or contact the National Association of Volunteer Bureaux, 29 Lower King's Road, Berkhamsted, Herts (tel: 04427 73311). Community Service Volunteers (tel: 01–278 6601) run several schemes using volunteers all over the country, including one specifically for older people called Retired and Senior Volunteer Programme. Most charities are able to make use of volunteers so your favourite local one may well offer you useful and interesting work.

4 MONEY FROM YOUR HOME

For most home owners, their home represents their most valuable asset. But there seems little point in owning a growing capital asset when the real need is for more income or for a capital sum. This chapter looks at how to turn that asset into cash.

People who own their house or flat have an enormous advantage when it comes to borrowing money. They can use their property as security for the loan. That means that if anything terrible happens and the payments are not met, the lender has the right to make you sell your home and pay them back out of the proceeds. So it's a procedure to use with care. But as you get older, you can use the security of your home to borrow larger amounts and guarantee full repayment on your death. While you continue to live, you just repay the interest on the loan.

There are two main ways in which such loans are used. The first is to raise capital, normally to pay for repairs to your house. These so-called 'maturity loans' are described in Chapter 9 of *Saga Rights Guide*, also by Paul Lewis in this series. The second, strangely, is to boost your income. There are two main ways in which you can use the capital value of your home to boost your income, both available only to older pensioners.

Retirement Annuities

Retirement annuities or home income plans turn part of the value of your home into an income for you until you die. When you die, part of the value of your home goes to repay the debt. You normally have to be at least seventy to participate. A couple normally needs a joint age of 145 and both partners must be at least seventy. The older you are, the better value these schemes seem. They are particularly good value for people who pay no tax, who lose some age allowance because their income is above £9,800, or who pay higher rates of tax.

The plans involve three steps. First, you take out a mortgage on your home. That simply means that you borrow an amount from a building society or insurance company secured on the value of your home. Normally, you can borrow up to £30,000. While you live, you just pay the interest on this loan. When you die, the capital is repaid from your estate. For a couple, that does not happen until the second member of the couple dies.

Second, the money you have borrowed is used to purchase an annuity. An annuity is simply an income for life from an insurance company in exchange for a capital sum. You give them the capital sum and they invest it. They keep the interest on it and the capital sum is theirs. In exchange, they pay you an amount each year for life. In effect the insurance company is gambling on your longevity. If you live a long time and collect the annuity for longer than they expected, then they will make a loss. If you live only a short time, they will make a profit. Insurance companies know exactly how long men and women of certain ages are expected to live and they calculate the money they pay you so that they will break even if you live longer than usual. So, overall, they never lose.

Third, you use the money from the annuity to do two things. You repay the interest on the loan. And the balance is yours to boost your income.

For example, Mrs Smith is seventy-five and has a small income, but just enough to pay tax. She uses her home, which is worth £50,000, to take out a home income plan. In exchange for a guarantee of £30,000 from the sale of her home when she dies, the insurance company gives her an annuity of £3,589 a year. Based on her age and sex, the Inland Revenue specify that £830 of that is income and the balance is repayment of capital. So she has to pay tax on £830. That comes to £224 and the insurance company deduct it before paying out the annuity. So her net annuity is:

	£	
Gross annuity	3,589	
less tax on £830	208	
Net annuity	3,381	3,381

Out of that amount she has to pay the interest on the loan of £30,000. That is at a fixed interest rate of 8.25% which makes it £2,475 a year. However, the Inland Revenue allow full tax relief on this interest and so the interest is reduced by 25%. She gets this even if she does not pay tax.

	£	
Loan interest @ 8.25%	2,475	
less tax relief @ 25%	619	
Interest after tax relief	1,856	1,856

So Mrs Smith's annuity brings in £3,381 a year and her loan costs her £1,856 a year. The difference is the amount she has to spend:

Net annual income	£1,525
Net weekly income	£29.32

Mrs Smith took out her plan with an insurance company. The rate of interest they charge on the loan is fixed at the current rate of 8.25%. That rate will not change whatever happens to interest rates. So she knows that her income from the plan will stay the same for the rest of her life. However, there are some schemes, mainly sold through building societies, that charge a variable rate of interest. These rates are generally higher but the annuity you receive is also greater. However, if interest rates rise, the net income you have left can be drastically reduced and, in extreme cases, may disappear altogether. Generally, a fixed rate gives you a slightly lower income but it is guaranteed for life. Variable rates give you a higher income initially, but it may vary and you run the risk of your income going down considerably.

How Much Will You Get?
Although Mrs Smith is typical, the income you would get depends on many factors. It could be much more or much less than she gets. The income from a home income plan depends on four main factors:

Your Age The older you are, the higher the income, because you will on average draw it for less time. The net annual income will be more than twice as much for someone of eighty than for someone of seventy.

Your Sex Women live longer than men and so get

a lower income. A woman will get about two thirds of the income of a man of the same age.

Marital Status A couple will receive less than a single person of the same age. The income continues until the *last* member of the couple dies, so on average a plan for a couple will pay out for longer than a plan for an individual. A couple will receive less than half the income given to a single man of the same age.

The Value of Your Home The most you can borrow is £30,000. And some companies will lend you only 60% of the value of your home.

In addition, your benefit from the scheme will depend on your other financial circumstances:

Income Support If you receive income support, the extra income from your home income plan will mean that your income support will be reduced or lost altogether. So a home income plan will not normally be worthwhile.

Housing Benefit If you get your rates reduced through housing benefit, this will be reduced by 20p for every £1 of your extra net income from the plan. In Mrs Smith's case that would reduce her housing benefit by 20% of £29.32, which works out at £5.86 a week. That may mean that a home income plan is not worthwhile.

Age Allowance If you lose *part* of your age allowance because your income is over £9,800, you will benefit particularly from an income plan because your total income for tax purposes will be reduced by the gross amount of the loan repayment before the tax relief is deducted. As a result your age allowance will increase.

Non-taxpayer If your income is too low to pay tax, you will benefit slightly more than someone who pays tax at the lowest rate. You will still get the interest on the loan reduced as if you paid tax. But you will not have to pay tax on all the extra income. However, the extra income from the plan may mean that you have to start paying some tax.

Higher Tax Allowances If you pay tax at the higher rate, you will benefit more than a standard rate taxpayer.

All these factors make it difficult to give any general rules about what people will receive. But Table 6 below shows typical net amounts for single men, single women and couples of various ages who pay tax at the standard rate of 25% from a loan of £30,000. The figures assume that the scheme is a fixed-interest-rate one and that you have taken out capital protection (this term is explained on page 47). If you get housing benefit or are on income support, your net gain will be less. If you pay higher rates of tax or no tax at all, or get a reduced age allowance because your income is over £9,800, your net gain will be more than shown (see also Chapter 5 for an explanation of tax over the age of sixty-five). If you borrow less than £30,000, your gain will be proportionally less.

Table 6
Net Gain from Home Income Plan by Age and Sex

Age	Single woman		Single man		Ages	Couple	
	Year £	Week £	Year £	Week £		Year £	Week £
70	1,037	19.94	1,456	28.00	72, 73	800	15.38
75	1,525	29.33	2,071	39.83	75, 75	1,070	20.58
80	2,192	42.15	2,874	55.27	80, 80	1,626	31.27

Source: Hinton and Wild

Problems

Unlocking some of the capital value of your home to provide an income late in life has great attractions. But there are problems to be faced as well.

Some property will not be accepted. Normally, it must be a freehold house or bungalow (not a flat) or a leasehold flat with at least sixty-five years left. Purpose-built retirement homes with a warden may not be accepted. The property must be in a reasonable state of repair. You will have to have an inspection and valuation at a fee related to the value of the property. The fee is normally repayable once you accept the plan. You will have to have the building properly insured against damage. You must not have tenants. The value of the property must be at least £22,000 (some companies specify more) and you will be lent between 60% and 80% of the value, depending on the company.

On average, the return over your life on your investment of £30,000 will be no more than £17,000 or £18,000. For example, at seventy-five Mrs Smith could expect to collect her £1,525 for about eleven years – a total of £16,775. When she dies, her heirs would inherit £30,000 less. However, any liability for inheritance tax (see Chapter 10), will be reduced as her estate is reduced by the amount of the loan. So they may not lose the full £30,000. In any case, it is sensible to explain your intentions to your heirs so that they are aware of the arrangements you are making.

However, it is not generally advisable for your heirs to try to act in the place of the insurance company and pay you the income themselves so that the value of your estate is kept intact. First, you may live a lot longer than the average! Second, few people have incomes which are secure enough to *guarantee* that they can honour a lifetime obligation to you. And third, you would lose a great deal of the independence which owning your own home gives you.

Capital Protection

One risk which you always take with one of these schemes is that you will die very soon after taking it out. If you die within a year, a home income plan which has given you £30 a week or so at a cost of £30,000 seems a very bad deal. So you can protect the amount of capital you lose if you die within three or four years of taking out the scheme. This capital protection means that you get a lower annuity and reduces your income by £3 or £4 a week. Capital protection is not normally needed for couples, as the chances of your both dying within three or four years is very small. However, if you do choose to have it, the cost will be low.

Remember that the income you get is fixed for life – £30 a week now will be worth far less in ten years' time. Even if inflation remains at 4% a year, the value of your income will have declined by a third in ten years.

If you want to move, you can simply transfer the home income plan as long as the value of the new property is enough to sustain the loan you have taken out. If you move to a property which is worth less, you can pay off some of the loan and reduce your outgoings. The value of the annuity remains the same, so your net income goes up.

Home Reversion Schemes

You may be offered another way of turning your home into cash. Home reversion schemes seem similar to home income plans but they are very different. You sell your property to the company offering the scheme. They give you a lump sum, usually of about half the value of the house though the amount varies with your age. And they allow you to live in the property at no charge until you die. The money they pay is not a loan, it is a cash payment in exchange for your home with you as a sitting tenant. So there is no loan interest to pay. You can do what you like with the lump sum, including buying an annuity.

Because you are giving up your title to your home, and there is no loan to repay, you generally get more from a home reversion scheme than from a home income plan. But your heirs get nothing. In exchange for about half the current value of your home when you take out the plan, the company gets the full market value of your home when you die.

On the whole, home reversion plans are not recommended unless you have no heirs.

Choosing a Scheme

If you want to consider a home income plan or a home reversion scheme, you should get independent financial advice. In theory, any broker should be able to give you independent advice and is obliged to do so. But there is one broker which specializes in these schemes: Hinton and Wild Home Plans, 374–378 Ewell Road, Tolworth, Surbiton, Surrey KT6 7BB (tel: 01–390 8166). In addition, the Abbey National Building Society now has a subsidiary called Abbey National Financial Services which offers independent advice on home income plans. They can be contacted through your local Abbey National Building Society or at the Head Office at 27 Baker Street, London W1M 2AA (tel: 01–486 5555). They will also advise on home reversion schemes if that is what you want.

5 INCOME TAX OVER SIXTY

Tax laws are complicated and there are special rules which apply to pensioners, making the subject particularly difficult. This chapter looks at the principal ways in which income tax affects retired people and widows. Chapter 6 looks at the interaction of tax and pensions.

Tax Allowances

For historical reasons, the tax year runs from 6 April in any year to 5 April the next. In each tax year everyone is allowed a certain amount of income before they start paying tax. This amount is called a tax allowance. Married men get a higher tax allowance than single people. And people aged sixty-five or more are normally given a higher tax allowance (called age allowance) than younger people. In 1987 the chancellor introduced an even higher age allowance for people over eighty, so people of that age can have slightly more income before they start paying tax.

Age Allowance

In 1988/89 the standard age allowance for people aged sixty-five to seventy-nine is £3,180 (£61.15 a week) for a single person and £5,035 (£96.83 a week) for a married man. The higher age allowance for people over eighty is £3,310 (£63.65) for a single person and £5,205 (£100.10) for a married man. People whose *total* income is less than these amounts should pay no tax at all. If your income is above these amounts, you will pay tax on the excess.

Age Limits

The standard age allowance is available if you, or your spouse, are aged sixty-five or more in the tax year. The over-eighties age allowance is available if you, or your spouse, are aged eighty or more in the tax year. Even if your birthday is on 5 April 1989, the last day of the current tax year, you can claim for the whole year. So if you *or* your spouse were born *before* 6 April 1924, you should get the standard age allowance. And if you *or* your spouse were born *before* 6 April 1909, you should get the over-eighties age allowance.

Women aged sixty to sixty-four do not receive the age allowance. They get the standard younger person's allowance which is £2,605 (£50.10 a week). A married man is allowed an income of £4,095 (£78.75 a week) before paying tax if both he and his wife are under sixty-five throughout the tax year.

Rate of Tax

The standard rate of tax on income above your allowances has been cut over a number of years and in 1988/89 it is 25%. People with incomes above about £22,000 a year pay a higher rate of tax. If your income on top of your tax allowances and allowable mortgage interest exceeds £19,300, you pay tax at 40% on the excess.

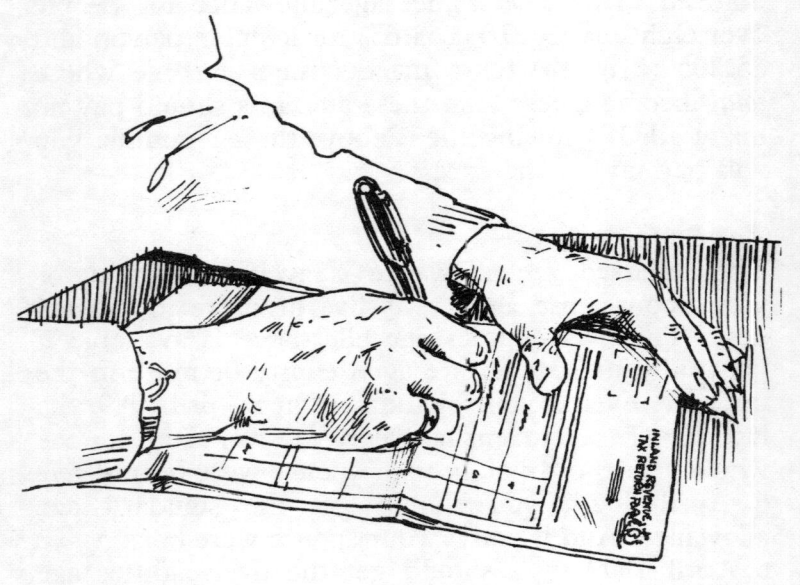

However, people over sixty-five pay a higher effective rate of tax if their income exceeds £10,600. If your income exceeds that amount, the age allowance itself is gradually reduced to the level of tax allowances for younger people.

To check if your income is above this amount you must first take off any mortgage interest you pay (including interest on a home income plan – see Chapter 4) or any covenant you may still pay in favour of, perhaps, a grandchild. In both cases you must take off the gross amount before the tax relief. If you have investment income where tax is already paid, such as from a building society, you must turn it into the equivalent gross income by multiplying by 1.33 (or, more accurately, dividing by 0.75). There is a full explanation of this process on page 54.

Once you have adjusted your income in this way,

for every £3 by which it exceeds £10,600, the age allowance is reduced by £2. So the standard age allowance is reduced to the normal younger person's allowance as income reaches £12,010 for a married man and £11,463 for a single person. For people over eighty, their age allowance is reduced to the normal single person's allowance as income reaches £12,265 for a married man and £11,658 for a single person. The effect of this rule is that you pay tax at almost 42% on the income between £10,600 and these limits.

For example, if your income is below £10,600, your tax is worked out as follows:

	£
Income	10,600
less tax allowance	3,180
taxable income	7,420
less tax @ 25% =	1,855
	5,565
add tax-free income	3,180
Total after-tax income	8,745

However, if your income exceeds £10,600, your tax allowance is reduced. The reduction is two thirds of the excess above £10,600. For example, an income of £10,900 is £300 above the limit. Two thirds of £300 is £200, so your tax allowance would be reduced by that amount, making it only £2,980. The effect on your net income is shown on page 54.

	£
Income	10,900
less reduced tax allowance	2,980
taxable income	7,920
less tax @ 25% =	1,980
	5,940
add tax-free income	2,980
Total after-tax income	8,920

The net income after tax is just £175 more as a result of a £300 rise in gross income. So you pay £125 in tax, making the effective rate of tax nearly 42%. That rate applies to all income between £10,600 and the upper limit for receiving an age allowance.

Investment Income
There is a further complexity about working out your entitlement to age allowance if you have income from money invested in a building society, bank deposit account, or in a local authority bond. All these investments now pay the interest net of basic rate tax.

To check whether your income is high enough for you to lose the age allowance, or to receive only a partial one, the Inland Revenue must know the size of your income before you pay tax. This amount is called your gross income. However, interest from a building society, a bank deposit account or a local authority is now paid net of tax, as if you had already paid the tax on it. So in order to assess your income fairly, the Revenue must work out what your gross income, before tax, would have been if the interest had been paid to you gross. This process is called 'grossing up'. To work out your grossed-up income you need to multiply the net income by 1.33 (to be exact, you divide by 0.75).

Suppose that your net income from the building society is £100. Then your grossed-up income is £100 × 1.33 = £133. You can see that figure is right by working out the tax due on £133. The tax due on £133 is £133 × 25% = £33, leaving a net income of £100. So you need £133 to give you the same net income as the £100 you get from the building society.

It is this grossed-up income you must use to see if you are entitled to a full age allowance or not. Of course, it is only income paid net of tax which you have to gross up in this way.

For example, Mary Higgins has a state pension of £43.95 and an occupational pension from her time as a civil servant of £555 a month. In addition she has £20,650 in a building society which, at 6.75% brings her in £1,393.88 a year. Does she get age allowance? If her actual income is added up, it comes to £10,339.28 which is less than the £10,600 limit, so she thinks she should get the full age allowance. But grossing up gives a different answer:

Annual income:	£
State pension £43.95 × 52 =	2,285.40
Superannuation £555 × 12 =	6,660.00
Interest £1,393.88 ÷ 0.75 =	1,858.51
	10,803.91

As her income is above the limit of £10,600, she gets a reduced age allowance. Table 7 (on page 56) shows the age allowance at various levels of income for single people and married men. In case you do not have a calculator, Table 8 (on page 57) shows grossed-up income at the new tax rate of 25%.

You can use the same process to work out the gross

Table 7
Age Allowance at Various Ages and Income Levels

Total income £	Tax allowance			
	65–79		80 or more	
	Single £	Married £	Single £	Married £
10,500	3,180	5,035	3,310	5,205
10,550	3,180	5,035	3,310	5,205
10,600	3,180	5,035	3,310	5,025
10,650	3,147	5,002	3,277	5,172
10,700	3,113	4,968	3,243	5,138
10,750	3,080	4,935	3,210	5,105
10,800	3,047	4,902	3,177	5,072
10,850	3,013	4,868	3,143	5,038
10,900	2,980	4,835	3,110	5,005
10,950	2,947	4,802	3,077	4,972
11,000	2,913	4,768	3,043	4,938
11,050	2,880	4,735	3,010	4,905
11,100	2,847	4,702	2,977	4,872
11,150	2,813	4,668	2,943	4,838
11,200	2,780	4,635	2,910	4,805
11,250	2,747	4,602	2,877	4,772
11,300	2,713	4,568	2,843	4,738
11,350	2,680	4,535	2,810	4,705
11,400	2,647	4,502	2,777	4,672
11,450	2,613	4,468	2,743	4,638
11,500	2,605	4,435	2,710	4,605
11,550	2,605	4,402	2,677	4,572
11,600	2,605	4,368	2,643	4,538
11,650	2,605	4,335	2,610	4,505
11,700	2,605	4,302	2,605	4,472
11,750	2,605	4,268	2,605	4,438
11,800	2,605	4,235	2,605	4,405
11,850	2,605	4,202	2,605	4,372
11,900	2,605	4,168	2,605	4,338
11,950	2,605	4,135	2,605	4,305
12,000	2,605	4,102	2,605	4,272
12,050	2,605	4,095	2,605	4,238
12,100	2,605	4,095	2,605	4,205
12,150	2,605	4,095	2,605	4,172
12,200	2,605	4,095	2,605	4,138
12,250	2,605	4,095	2,605	4,105
12,300	2,605	4,095	2,605	4,095
12,350	2,605	4,095	2,605	4,095
12,400	2,605	4,095	2,605	4,095

Table 8
Equivalent Gross Incomes
(basic rate of tax = 25%)

Income after basic rate tax £	Grossed-up income £
1	1.33
2	2.67
3	4.00
4	5.33
5	6.67
6	8.00
7	9.33
8	10.67
9	12.00
10	13.33
20	27.67
30	40.00
40	53.33
50	66.67
60	80.00
70	93.33
80	106.67
90	120.00
100	133.33
200	266.67
300	400.00
400	533.33
500	666.67
600	800.00
700	933.33
800	1,066.67
900	1,200.00
1,000	1,333.33
2,000	2,666.67
3,000	4,000.00
4,000	5,333.33
5,000	6,666.67
8,000	10,666.67
10,000	13,333.33

amount of the interest on a loan on your house.

Do remember that you should not have money invested in a building society or a bank deposit account if you do not pay any tax at all. There is more information on the investments you should consider in Chapters 7 and 8.

Widows

The tax position of widows is not only complicated but unique. In the tax year in which your husband died, you are taxed as a married couple until the date of his death. That means that a full married man's allowance is given for your joint income from 6 April up to the date your husband died. For the rest of the tax year, until 5 April, you are taxed as a single person and receive a full single person's allowance. You also get an extra tax allowance, called widow's bereavement allowance. It makes up your total tax allowances to the same amount as a married man's tax allowance for the balance of the tax year in which your husband dies. So you and your late husband get the equivalent of two full married man's tax allowances in the tax year of his death.

The bereavement allowance is also given to you in the next tax year. However, if you remarry before the start of the second tax year, you do not receive the second year of the widow's bereavement allowance. Remarriage cannot affect the first year's allowance. If you intend to remarry quite soon after your husband's death, it may be worth delaying the wedding until after the start of the tax year on 6 April to avoid losing the second year's relief which is worth £7.16 a week.

In 1988/89 the tax allowance for a widow who receives bereavement allowance will be the single person's allowance of £2,605 plus the extra bereavement allowance of £1,490, making £4,095 altogether. You get the full annual allowance no matter how late in the tax year your husband dies.

A widower is not given the widow's bereavement allowance. He is simply taxed as a married man for the whole of the tax year in which his wife dies.

Over and Under Sixty-five

Widow's bereavement allowance is the same for women aged over sixty-five as for younger women. There is no special age allowance. So their tax allowance is not made up fully to the married man's age allowance. It is the sum of the single person's age allowance and the widow's bereavement allowance, so it is £4,670.

Women, including widows, who are under sixty-five for the whole tax year do not receive the single person's age allowance. If their widow's bereavement allowance has run out, they get the normal single person's tax allowance of £2,605 (£50.10 a week). Remember that you can obtain the age allowance for the whole tax year, even if your sixty-fifth birthday is right on the last day of the tax year, 5 April.

The interaction of age and the bereavement allowance means that a widow can obtain four different amounts of tax allowance in the first two years of widowhood. They are set out below.

WIDOW'S TAX ALLOWANCE

	Bereavement allowance	
	Yes	No
	£	£
Age		
Under sixty-five	4,095	2,605
Over sixty-five	4,670	3,180

Tell the Tax Office

The tax position of older people and widows can be very complicated. So it is important that you should contact the tax office if you think that you are not being given the correct allowances. In particular, people over eighty should check that they are being given the new over-eighties' allowance and people whose income may have been high enough for them to lose the age allowance in the past should check that it is being applied correctly this year. Married women with their own pension should check that this is being offset against their wife's earned income allowance.

Self-employed

If you are intending to do occasional work for more than one employer, you should consider becoming self-employed. The tax advantages are considerable. You can offset all your expenses, including part of your car costs, against your earnings and, if you set aside a small part of your home to do your books and make your arrangements, you can set a proportion of your heating costs and other home expenses against your tax too. After the first two tax years, your earnings are taxed on what is called 'a preceding year basis' so that your earnings in 1988/89 will be taxed in 1989/90. And you can delay the tax even further by fixing your own accounting year to end on, say, 30 April. In that case your profits are taxed in the year after the tax year in which your accounting year ends. So your profits on your year 1988/89 will be taxed in 1990/91.

This system does not work well when your income

starts to decline as your tax will relate to earlier, more profitable years. In that case it is probably best to stop trading altogether and take advantage of the concessions when a business ceases. If you are thinking of earning a reasonable amount through self-employment, it is worth consulting a tax advisor about tax in the first two years, when to fix your year end, and what to do when you want to retire completely!

Tax on Savings

Nowadays, interest paid on all bank deposit accounts and by local authorities is paid in the same way as building societies have traditionally paid interest. You receive the interest with the basic rate tax already paid for you. The institutions pay the tax to the Government on the interest earned by all their savers. Many savers do not pay tax (a lot of them are children with small savings), so the amount of tax paid averaged out over all savers is less than the standard rate of tax. This year banks, building societies and local authorities will pay tax on your behalf at 23¼% on the interest you earn instead of 25%. So your net interest should be that bit higher than if you were paid it gross and then paid the tax yourself at 25%.

To compare interest rates paid 'gross' and 'net' you have to convert one into the other. To convert net to gross you multiply by 1.33 (or, more accurately, divide by 0.75). To convert gross to net you multiply by 0.75. The recent reductions in the basic rate of tax affect the value of interest paid net of tax: interest of 6% net of 30% tax is clearly more valuable than 6% net of 25% tax. At 30% tax, the 6% is equivalent to a taxable interest rate of 8.57% (6 divided by 0.7). At

25% tax it is equivalent to 8% (6 divided by 0.75). The difference is probably not large enough to be likely to change your investment decisions yet. But if this process of reducing the standard rate of tax continues, then it may be significant in the future.

This system of paying interest net of basic rate tax has some advantages, but it is not fair for those who do not pay tax. They cannot claim back the tax paid on their behalf.

Although interest from a building society, bank, or local authority is free of *basic rate* tax, if you pay the higher rate of tax you have to pay the extra tax above the basic rate on it. So your interest always has to be shown on your tax return.

If you do not pay tax, or you want your interest paid 'gross' for some other reason, National Savings accounts which traditionally have paid interest gross will continue to do so, including the investment account and income and deposit bonds. Remember that the first £70 interest from the National Savings Bank ordinary account is tax-free anyway. It is often advisable to have some money in National Savings to ensure that your tax allowances are fully utilized. There is more information about National Savings and using your tax allowances in Chapter 7.

Alternatively, most high street banks have branches in the Channel Islands where you can deposit money and get the interest paid gross. The interest can be credited direct to a mainland bank account if you wish. You should ask your bank manager if you are interested in one of these accounts.

New Investment Income

New sources of investment income are taxed in a strange and confusing way. Normally, tax on investment income is due in the year after the income is received. However, when a source of investment income ends, by law no tax can be collected after it has ceased. These two rules together would mean that a year's investment income was never taxed. So the Inland Revenue adopt a special rule and tax one of the early years *twice*.

The method works in this way. In the first two years, you are normally taxed on the income in the year you receive it. In the third year, you are normally taxed on the income received in the previous year. So you are taxed twice on the same second year's income. However, you can choose to pay tax on your third year's income instead in that year. But if you make that choice, then in the fourth year you must be taxed on the previous year's income – that is, the third year's income.

So the choice you face is whether to be taxed twice on the second or the third year's income. The choice is yours, so clearly you will choose the year when you had the least income to be taxed. Thereafter, you continue to be taxed on the previous year's income. You can exercise this choice up to six years after the year in question.

Similar provisions apply when the source of income ceases. One of the final years' income is not taxed at all. Normally it is the last but one year which is omitted, so that the final tax bill is on the final year's tax. But the Revenue, not you, can choose to tax the last-but-one year instead of the final year if they wish. They usually choose to do so to increase your tax bill.

6 TAX AND PENSIONS

Your retirement pension counts as part of your income, so you can have only a limited income on top of it before you start paying tax. This chapter looks at the interaction of tax and pensions, including widow's pension and foreign pensions. Chapter 5 explains the terms used and the basic principles of income tax for people over sixty-five.

Income on Top of Basic Pension

In 1988/89 the age allowance is £3,180 (£61.15 a week) for a single person aged sixty-five to seventy-nine. The basic retirement pension is £41.15. So you can have £20 income a week on top of the basic retirement pension before you start paying tax. The figures for a married man where he and his wife are under eighty and one of them is sixty-five or more is £30.93. For people over eighty, the figures are £22.50 (single) and £34.20 (married) on top of the basic retirement pension. A single woman aged under sixty-five throughout the tax year who does not get the age allowance can only have about £8.95 a week on top of the basic pension before she starts paying tax.

If you have extra amounts on top of your basic pension, such as graduated pension, earnings related additional pension, or extra pension for postponing retirement, then obviously you can have less other income before you start paying tax. But if you still have dependent children, the extra pension you get for them is tax-free.

It is possible, especially for single women under sixty-five, that the tax allowance will not be enough to cover your state pension including the graduated, additional and extra pension you may have added on to the basic pension. So you could end up paying tax on your state pension alone.

The Inland Revenue have a special procedure for dealing with this problem. Usually they will be aware, through your local tax office, that you have left work at pension age. In most cases they will write to you enquiring about your sources of income after retirement. They will also know the date on which your state pension starts and the amount of it from a form P46 which the DHSS issues to the revenue for every pension award. If your pension seems likely to exceed your tax allowance, they will assess the tax due and ask you to pay it in four equal quarterly instalments starting thirty days after the assessment is made. If those payments will cause you any hardship, they will be prepared to allow a more frequent payment of smaller amounts. You should write to them if you want to negotiate such a deal.

You should note that the Inland Revenue ignore sums of tax due of less than £40 in a year which they say are not worth collecting. So your total income in the tax year can exceed your tax allowance by £148 (£2.84 a week) before any tax will normally be collected. However, if you fill in a tax return for any reason, they will collect all the tax due, even if it is less than £40.

Sometimes a married woman can reduce her husband's tax bill by claiming her own pension on her own contribution record rather than on his. If she does this, she can then set her own pension against another tax allowance called wife's earned income allowance. This allowance is £2,605 (£50.10 a week) and it applies only to earned income and a company or state pension paid as a result of the woman's own earnings (or to a retirement or widow's pension paid on the basis of her late or ex-husband's contributions if she has remarried). It is in addition to her husband's age allowance. So it will mean that her own pension is tax-free unless she also still earns money or has a pension from her job which exceeds the allowance.

Many women do not know if they are entitled to any pension of their own. Even if they do, such a pension would often be less than the married woman's pension they get from their husband's contributions so they do not bother to claim it. Both pensions cannot be paid in full on top of each other. However, a woman can claim the part which is hers and, usually, it is paid instead of just part of her married woman's pension.

For example, if your married woman's pension were £24.75 and you claimed a pension on your own contributions of £10.70, your married woman's pension would be reduced by that amount to £14.05. You would still get £24.75 altogether. But the £10.70 would be completely tax-free unless you have earnings or a pension from a job which, together with your £10.70, exceeds £46.63 a week. So even if your own state pension is small, it is still worth claiming it if your husband pays tax. The tax saving on a £10.70 pension is £2.68.

Unfortunately, the position is more complicated for older couples. If both partners reached pension age before 6 April 1979, the woman must choose between her own pension and the pension paid on her husband's contributions. She can get one *or* the other. If she chooses her own pension, she loses the whole of her married woman's pension. Her pension is usually less than the married woman's pension, so it is not usually worth claiming it unless the tax relief exceeds the loss – in other words, unless her own pension is more than 75% of the one due on her husband's contributions which normally means that it must be more than £18.56 a week.

However, this more restrictive rule does not apply if *either* she was born *after* 5 April 1919, *or* her husband was born *after* 5 April 1914. Then it is always better to claim her own pension if her husband pays tax. Moreover, the rule does not seem to be applied to women who got their pension because of the final abolition of the half-test in 1984. Women born before 6 April 1919 who received a letter from the DHSS in 1985 informing them that they had been given a pension in their own right and that the letter was 'for tax-relief purposes only' can use the letter to ensure their husband gets the tax relief whenever he was born.

Details of how married women can sometimes claim pensions of £10.29 a week and more from contributions paid over forty years ago are in a new edition of the leaflet *Pensions from the Forties*, available from Saga Money Guide, *Saga Magazine*, Saga Building, Middelburg Square, Folkestone, Kent CT20 1AZ.

Widows or divorced women who have remarried over the age of sixty should note that they can set their retirement pension paid on their late husband's contributions against their wife's earned income tax allowance.

If you are self-employed, the income that counts for tax is not the current year's income (see Chapter 5).

People registered as blind receive an extra tax allowance of £540.

Tax on Company Pensions

Income from your company pension is taxable. Normally it is taxed at source before you receive it and the Inland Revenue give the pension payer a tax code for you so that they can calculate the tax due. You will be sent a copy of the notice of coding which shows how the tax code is calculated.

The tax code is worked out as follows. Your tax allowances are the amount of money you can have each year without paying any tax. Your DHSS retirement pension is taxable, so the Revenue deduct the amount of that from your allowances to leave the amount of income you can have before you pay tax. For example, your age allowance may be £3,180 and your retirement pension £44 a week or £2,288 a year. £3,180 minus £2,288 equals £892. That means you can have £892 a year on top of your retirement pension without paying tax. The figure is converted to a tax code by knocking off the last number, making 89. The code is then used to calculate the tax due on the pension you get from your job. All it means is that you pay tax on the amount above the £890 that remains from your allowances.

Your code consists of numbers and letters: for example, the code above would be 89P. The letters show the sort of tax allowance you get:

L   Single person under sixty-five.
H   Married man, both he and his wife under sixty-five.
P   Single person's age allowance, aged sixty-five to seventy-nine.
V   Married man's age allowance, both he and his wife aged less than eighty and one at least sixty-five.

T   Partial age allowance because your earnings are
        over £10,600 *or* over-eighties' age allowance *or*
        you have asked the tax office to keep your tax
        allowance secret.
OT   All your pension is to be taxed because your
        allowances are all used up.
F   Your state benefits come to more than your tax-
        free allowances so your company pension has to
        be taxed at a higher rate to ensure that the tax
        due on the state pension is collected. Newly
        retired people with large earnings related addi-
        tional pension paid with their basic pension may
        well have this coding. See Chapter 2 for more
        details of these pensions.
NT   No tax is to be deducted at all.

If you have a job as well as a pension, you may see
'BR' on your tax code which means 'Deduct tax at
basic rate'. D0, indicates that tax has to be deducted
at the higher rate.

Tax on Foreign Pensions

Income from pensions paid by countries outside the
UK, whether from a foreign state or a foreign
company, is liable for tax in the UK. That is true
even if the pension is paid abroad into an account in a
foreign bank and used only abroad – on holiday, for
example.

The value of a foreign pension changes with the
rate of exchange. The pension should be taxed on its
actual value in sterling when you receive it. However,
the Inland Revenue may offer to tax it on the basis of
an average rate of exchange over the tax year. You
can accept that method or, if you think it would be

better for you, insist that the tax is levied on the actual value you receive in sterling each month.

By a special concession, only 90% of the value of a foreign pension is liable for tax. So the sterling value is reduced by 10% before tax is calculated.

Foreign pensions are taxed under the same system as new investment income. Under this method, which is described more fully in Chapter 5, the money received in either the second or the third year is taxed twice. You can choose which year has this double tax.

Tax on a Widow's Pension

Most widows receive a widow's pension. Women widowed under sixty, and some widowed over that age, also get a lump sum of £1,000 called widow's payment. The widow's pension is taxable, but the widow's payment is not. The income you obtain from the pension uses up a lot of your tax allowances. So the income you can have on top of the basic widow's pension before you pay tax is fairly limited, especially after the end of the tax year in which your husband died.

In the first tax year, the amount you can get on top of your pension before you pay tax depends on the month in which your husband died. After his death, you receive the whole annual tax allowance, however close it is to the end of the tax year on 5 April. So if your husband dies close to the end of the tax year – say, in February or March – you qualify for a whole year's tax allowance to cover just a few weeks' income. It is likely, therefore, that you will not need to pay any tax at all yourself in that tax year.

However, if he dies early in the tax year – say, in late April or May – you will get the same tax allowance over almost a whole year. So the earlier in the tax year that your husband dies, the less income you will be able to have on top of your pension before you start to pay tax. If your husband dies right at the start of the tax year, you will be able to have only about £37.60 a week on top of your pension before you start paying tax if you are under sixty-five. If you are over sixty-five, you will be able to have more income on top of your benefit, about £48.66 on top of your pension before you start paying tax. But if your husband dies later in the tax year, you will be able to have much more than these amounts.

In the second year the position is a bit simpler. If you are under sixty-five, you will be able to have £37.60 a week on top of your pension without paying tax. If you are aged sixty-five or over, the figure is £48.66 assuming that you do not get widow's allowance. After the second tax year, you will just get a single person's tax allowance. You will then be able to have £8.95 on top of your basic pension if you are under sixty-five and £20 if you are aged sixty-five or more. Table 9 summarizes the position.

Remember that each amount is the average over the year on top of the basic widow's benefits.

Because your widow's benefits take up most of your tax allowances, if you do earn any extra money you

Table 9
Weekly Tax-free Income on Top of Widow's Benefit

Age	Tax year husband dies (£)	Next tax year (£)	Tax year after that (£)
Under 65	At least 36.70	36.70	8.95
Over 65	At least 48.66	48.66	20.00

will find that your employer will have to tax most of it at the standard rate of 25p in the £. If you earn more than £41 a week and you are under sixty, you will have to pay National Insurance contributions as well. Once you reach sixty, you do not have to pay National Insurance. You should check to make sure you do not pay any contributions on any payday *after* your sixtieth birthday.

If you receive a pension from your husband's old employer, it will normally have tax at 25p in the £ taken off it before you get it. You may be able to claim some of this tax back if you have no other income.

The calculations about how much tax you pay as a widow can be complicated. Even the Inland Revenue may make mistakes from time to time. So you should fill in a tax return each year to make sure you have paid the right amount of tax. Ask for one from your tax office.

7 NATIONAL SAVINGS

In the past, little more than patriotism has attracted people to National Savings. But today National Savings is competing hard for your money. For most people there is a worthwhile investment package waiting.

Tax-free Interest

Some National Savings products offer interest or gains which are completely free of tax. These are different from investments in building societies and banks, which pay interest to you as if the basic rate tax had been paid. On the latter investments, higher rates of tax still have to be paid if you are liable for them and the 'grossed-up' value can affect your age allowance. Neither of those problems (which are explained in Chapter 5) arises with National Savings investments. However, because they are free of tax, the rates of interest paid on these investments are lower than for other National Savings investments. They are all ideal for retired taxpayers, especially those who pay the higher rate of tax or whose income is just above £10,600.

Savings Certificates
You can invest between £25 and £1000 in the current issue of savings certificates (the 33rd, though this may have been withdrawn by the time this book is

published). As the investment market changes, the state withdraws one issue of certificates from sale and introduces another. But the same principle applies to them all. Your investment grows each year and the growth is re-invested. At the end of five years you can cash the whole investment. The maximum £1,000 invested in the 33rd issue will be worth £1,402.55 after five years, which is equivalent to an interest rate of 7%. If you are buying the certificates by cashing in earlier certificates, you can invest more. If you cash in the certificates early, you get a lower rate of interest and it is paid only for each complete three months you have held the certificates. You may have to wait a week or two for the money to be sent to you. If you cash in the certificates in the first year, you get no interest at all. If you leave the certificates uncashed after the full term, interest is paid at a variable rate announced by the Government. The income from certificates is free of all income tax and capital gains tax. It does not have to be entered on your tax return and it does *not* affect your age allowance.

If you pay the higher rate of tax (or lose some of your age allowance) and can bear to lock some money up for five years, National Savings certificates may be attractive to you. They are generally *not* a good deal for non-taxpayers.

You buy certificates at a post office and you can obtain a leaflet about them there.

Index-linked Certificates

Index-linked certificates were introduced during the period of high inflation in the seventies. The rate of inflation was then much higher than the rate of interest you could normally earn. So savings declined in value. In 1975 the Government introduced index-linked certificates for pensioners where the interest rate was guaranteed to match the decline in value caused by inflation.

However, the rate of inflation fell and was soon below interest rates again. So the attraction of index-linked certificates declined. However, the Government made them more attractive by offering bonuses. The current issue, the 4th, offers a bonus of more than 4% on top of inflation over five years.

The income from index-linked certificates, like that from ordinary savings certificates, is free of all income tax and capital gains tax. And there are similar penalties for cashing them in early.

If you worry that inflation will rise again within five years, these certificates may be attractive to you, especially if you pay tax at the higher rate or lose some age allowance because of your income.

You buy these index-linked certificates at a post office and you can obtain a leaflet about them there.

Premium Bonds
Premium bonds were introduced in 1956. Interest is not paid to investors directly. Instead it goes into a prize draw and the holders of the bonds are eligible for the prizes. Today 25 million people hold at least one bond. Most prizes are £50 but the top monthly prize is now £250,000 and there are weekly prizes of £100,000, £50,000 and £25,000.

Although the premium bond is a lottery, your capital is not at risk. You can withdraw your investment intact at any time. The lottery simply determines how the interest is shared out. At the moment, the total premium bond investment earns interest annually at 7%. That amounts to over £11 million a month. Every bond has a fixed chance of 11,000 to 1 in each draw of winning *something*. So if

you have £100 invested, you have a chance of 110 to 1 each month and will, on average, win something every nine years or so. Of course, if you had the maximum £10,000 invested, you could expect on average to win something almost every month.

The interest rate of 7% free of all tax makes premium bonds comparable to building society premium accounts for basic-rate taxpayers and rather better for people paying tax at higher rates. But the main attraction of premium bonds is that they are fun. It is not very interesting to earn £7 a year on an investment of £100. But it is very exciting to know that you have the chance of winning £250,000! Your £7 unpaid interest is your stake in Britain's national lottery.

There is a minimum investment of £10 and a new bond does not go into the draw for three clear calendar months after purchase. So, for example, a bond bought at any time in January is entered in the May draw. You can cash a bond in at any time.

The bonds are selected by a machine called ERNIE. The numbers drawn are thoroughly checked for randomness by an independent auditor and there are no 'lucky' or unlucky numbers. You can arrange to go and see ERNIE and have its workings explained if you contact the Prize Draw Supervisor, Bonds and Stock Office, Blackpool FY3 9YP (tel: 0253 66151).

If you like a gamble, then it is worth having some money in premium bonds, especially if you pay tax.

You can buy premium bonds at a post office and at banks. There is a special leaflet about them entitled *Your Questions on ERNIE*.

Interest Paid Gross

National Savings offer one of the few safe investments which still pay interest 'gross'. Building societies, local authorities and banks all now pay interest as if you had already paid basic rate income tax on it. If you do not pay tax, it is advisable to have some money invested in National Savings where the interest is paid gross.

For example, a married man of sixty-six gets the age allowance of £5,035. If his retirement pension is £65.90 and his company pension is £12.33, his annual income is £4,068. That means that he can have £967 free of tax. So he could invest enough capital in National Savings which pay interest gross to give him £967 and put the rest in a building society or in a tax-free National Savings product.

Income Bonds
An income bond gives you a monthly income from your investment. The bonds are sold in multiples of £1,000, but you must invest at least £2,000 and the

interest rate at the time of writing is 10.5%. The income is paid monthly and can be credited direct to a bank or building society account. The interest rate is not fixed so your income will change as the rate goes up or down. You must give three months' notice to cash in a bond and you can cash them in only in multiples of £1,000. If you cash in within the first year, you get only half the interest rate.

Index-linked bonds are similar except that the income is calculated at 8% in the first year and then in each subsequent year it is increased so that your monthly income keeps pace with inflation. The bonds are sold in multiples of £1,000, but there is a minimum holding of £5,000. The capital is not protected against inflation. After ten years the capital is repaid to you if you have not already withdrawn it.

You can obtain the forms and addressed envelope to apply for bonds from a post office where you will also find leaflets about them.

Deposit Bonds

Deposit bonds are similar to income bonds but the interest is not paid monthly. Instead it accumulates until the bond is cashed. Each year the interest earned to date is credited and begins to earn interest itself. However, the interest is liable for tax each year, even though you do not withdraw it. The bonds are in units of £50 but there is minimum holding of £100. They can be cashed in multiples of £50 on three months' notice.

You can obtain the forms and addressed envelope to apply for bonds from a post office where you will also find leaflets about them.

Investment Account

The National Savings investment account is similar to

a building society account. You can invest any amount from £5 to £100,000. The interest rate varies but is currently 10%. You can make withdrawals at one month's notice. The interest is liable to income tax if your income is high enough.

You open the account at your local post office.

Ordinary Account
The National Savings ordinary account is similar to a bank deposit account. You can invest any amount from £1 to £10,000. You must keep a balance of at least £500 throughout 1988 to earn the higher interest rate of 5%. If it falls below that amount in any month, the interest rate is only 2½% for that month. These interest rates are fixed until 31 December 1988 but may change after that. You can withdraw up to £100 on demand at a post office and larger amounts within a few days by post. The first £70 interest in the tax year is free of income tax. Interest above that amount is liable to income tax if your income is high enough.

You can make deposits and withdraw up to £100 on demand at most post offices and you open the account at your local post office.

8 STOCKS AND SHARES

If you do not fancy the extreme safety of National Savings, you may want to be more adventurous with your money. This chapter looks at some of the choices.

Government Stock

Government stock (often called 'gilt-edged' stock) is an odd but interesting form of investment. It is best explained by taking a specific investment. For example, 9½% Treasury stock 1999 was offered for sale in lots of £100. The Government guarantees to pay 9½% interest on each £100 of stock for each year until 1999. At that time the Government will redeem the stock at its face value of £100.

You can obtain a list of all the current stock from the post office and you will see that there are a whole range of redemption dates, from 1988 to 2016, and a wide range of interest rates from less than 5% up to 15½%. Obviously, interest rates of over 15% are very attractive. But you cannot buy stock at its face value of £100 after its first date of issue. Instead, you have to buy stock at its market value. For example, the 15½% Treasury stock 1998 might sell for £135 a unit. So you would buy a unit of £100 for £135 and get interest of 15½% on the £100. Thus you would receive interest of £15.50 for your investment of £135, representing a crude rate of interest of about 11.5%.

However, if you keep the stock until its redemption date in 1998, you get only £100 for the stock for which you paid £135 in 1988. So over the next ten years you lose £35 which reduces the real interest rate to about 10%. (The calculation of this 'redemption yield' is very complex and not at all obvious.)

The current prices of all Government stock are given in the finance pages of the serious newspapers together with an indication of the interest rate (though not all give the rate taking account of the capital loss or gain at redemption). Some stock is cheaper than its nominal value because it is paying a very low rate of interest. And some stock has no redemption date. War Loan 3½%, for example, now sells at about £37 for £100 of stock. The Government has never fixed a date for its redemption at face value and it seems unlikely that it will do so. Many people who bought this stock for its face value in the war feel very upset that the Government will not repay them the face value while offering such a low rate of return. So they hang on to their stock in the hope that the Government will change its mind.

Interest is paid half-yearly gross. You have to declare the interest on your tax return and it is taxable. Bonds held for at least a year are exempt from capital gains tax.

You can obtain the form to invest in the stock from a post office. Send the completed form with a cheque to the Bonds and Stock Office in Blackpool (address on page 77). They charge a small commission.

Local Authority Bonds

Many local authorities raise money by inviting the public to lend to them and offering good rates of interest. However, the money is normally tied up for the whole period of the loan, usually between one and ten years, though some shorter-term investments are possible.

You can obtain the best current rates over the telephone from Sterling Brokers on 01–407 2767, or they will send you a comprehensive list of all local authority investment offers if you send £2.50 to them at Colechurch House, 1 London Bridge Walk, London SE1 2SS. If you want to invest in the current best offer over the telephone, they will give you the contact number at the relevant local authority.

The interest is paid net of basic-rate tax as with a building society account. This type of investment is best suited to basic-rate taxpayers who can tie up some money for a fixed period of time.

The Stock Market

All the investments referred to above are safe. You cannot lose your capital. The same is true of putting your money in a bank or building society. Returns are not spectacular, but you take no real risk with your hard-earned cash. The stock market is different. Your capital is always at risk. Your investment of £1,000 could be worth nothing in a year's time or it could be worth £10,000. The stock market crash of October 1987 has shown people how dangerous investing in it can be. The value of shares of many sound companies fell by half overnight. Investing in shares yourself is a gamble and, if you are going to make a consistently good return on your money, it is a very time-consuming hobby. But if you have the time and the nerve for it, you may do well.

There is a growing market in cheaply produced

periodicals which allegedly give you inside information to help you make money on the stock market. These periodicals (commonly called tip-sheets) are not cheap – £100 a year is typical – so you have to do well from them to make it worthwhile buying them.

If you want to invest in shares, you can still go through a stockbroker who will charge a commission which can be 1% to 1½% of the amount invested for small deals. The fixed fees were abolished in 1986. In addition there is ½% stamp duty charged on any purchase you make. Alternatively, you can now buy shares through other intermediaries. They often offer you no commission deals, but their selling prices are dearer and their buying prices less than those of a traditional stockbroker. (This difference between the buying and selling price of a share is called the 'spread'.) They advertise in the financial pages of newspapers or magazines. Some department stores now operate 'share shops' where you can buy and sell shares easily. Occasionally, these intermediaries have gone bust with client's money. But that should be less of a problem since the Financial Services Act has come into force (see Chapter 9). Whoever you deal through, remember that their fee has to be taken into account when you assess your profit or loss.

The return on shares comes in two forms. First, the share itself may grow in value. A share for which you paid £2 may become worth £4 if the company does well. You can then sell the share for that higher price, but remember that there will be commission to pay and the price you can sell for is always less than the quoted buying price. If you do really well and you make a capital gain of more than £5,000 in a year, you will have to pay capital gains tax (see Chapter 10).

Second, the company may pay a dividend to shareholders. This dividend is paid net of basic rate

tax but you can reclaim the tax if you are a non-taxpayer. In addition some companies offer perks to shareholders, especially larger ones, in the form of a discount on buying the products or services they provide.

Unit Trusts

If you want to have money in the stock market but do not want the complications of dealing yourself, one alternative is to let professionals do the investing for you by buying units in a unit trust. A unit trust is simply a fund of money managed by professionals who buy and sell shares in companies. The investor buys a share (or unit) of this fund and then shares in the growth (or loss) of the fund as a whole. There are over a thousand different unit trusts, some of them general funds where the risks and returns are lower. But more and more funds are offering specialized investments such as Japanese or new British companies, and these may offer more spectacular results – in either direction! Many showed considerable growth in 1987 despite the crash of October. When choosing a unit trust, remember that a previous year's performance does not guarantee this year's.

You buy units direct from the trust. They are widely advertised. There is ½% stamp duty charged on any purchase you make.

Another alternative is buy a bond from an insurance company. These investments offer no guaranteed return and are for a fixed term of one year or more. But if you pick the right one, it can offer spectacular capital growth.

Other Investments

If you start looking for investment opportunities, you are bound to come across someone offering you, or appearing to offer you, a guaranteed and fantastically high return on your investment. Don't take it! At worst they are crooks who will take your money and run. At best, their advertisement is carefully worded to mislead you into believing that you can make an overnight fortune. If there were an easy way to make money, they would be doing it themselves, not bothering with advertisements to offer it to you.

However, some investments do offer the prospect of spectacular gains and are not crooked – just high-risk. In many cases you would be as wise to put the money on a horse you fancy. Such investments are typically not in real commodities, like shares or coffee beans, but in the price of commodities in the future; they are called 'futures' or 'options'. They are for professional investors.

9 FINANCIAL ADVICE AND PROTECTION

It is difficult to know where to go for financial advice. But a new law should mean that you can be sure the advice you get is in your best interests. This chapter explains your rights and how to complain when things go wrong.

Consumer Protection

The present Government has tried to encourage people to invest their money and to take an active interest in the stock market and making provision for their retirement. As part of this change, they introduced the Financial Services Act to try to regulate the growing numbers of financial advisors and intermediaries and to give the consumer of financial products protection from bad advice, unfair trading and dishonesty. The Act comes into force in 1988.

As with any system of regulation, those who are regulated like it less than those whom it protects. Many individual insurance brokers have decided to cease trading and there is a fear that the large companies will dominate more and more of the investment advice business.

Investment

The Act covers only investment businesses. Investments include all the things covered in Chapters 7 and 8, such as unit trusts, stocks and shares, futures options and National Savings products, as well as insurance schemes which involve investment (but not simple insurance of property or term life assurance) and pension schemes linked directly to investments (personal pension plans but not company pensions).

Anyone who earns any part of their living by selling any of these products or advising people on where to invest is carrying on an investment business. And anyone carrying on an investment business must be registered with a body approved by the Securities and Investments Board (SIB) which has been given its powers by the secretary of state for trade and industry.

So far there are five approved bodies, but the two you are most likely to come across are called the Financial Intermediaries, Managers, and Brokers Regulatory Association (FIMBRA) and the Life Assurance and Unit Trust Regulatory Organization (LAUTRO). Their addresses are in the Appendix at the end of this book.

Anyone who offers you investment advice as a business must be registered with one of these self-regulating bodies or the SIB. If they are not registered, they are committing a criminal offence if they carry on with their investment business after April 1988. They also commit a criminal offence if they encourage anyone to invest by making false or misleading statements.

The Act separates everyone in the investment business into two quite distinct groups. This process is called 'polarization'. No individual or company can be in both groups at the same time. One group consists of the tied agents who sell the financial products of just one company – an example would be a salesman for a major insurance company. They are allowed to sell only that company's products and are not allowed to compare them, favourably or otherwise, with anyone else's products. They must make it clear to you that they are tied agents.

The other group contains the independent financial advisors (a term you often see nowadays). They are independent of any company that makes or sells financial products and they have very strict obligations to act in your best interest. They cannot deal in the products of just one or two or even a few companies.

This division of people is very useful for the consumer. But it can have extraordinary results. For example, bank managers used to be a good source of advice. But now they will normally be able to advise you only on their own bank's products. They must tell you that is the limit of their advice. And, among their bank's own products, they must find the best to suit your circumstances. However, if you want to consider other products, they will not be able to advise you at all. Very often they will refer you to a separate but associated company which is acting as an independent financial advisor. One exception to this rule is NatWest where the managers are acting as independent financial advisors.

In addition to this strict division between tied agents and independent advisors, there are strict rules about how an investment business is to be carried out. They have to ensure that they take account of your circumstances and try to find you the best deal from the entire market to suit your purposes and individual needs. They must give you enough information to enable you to come to an informed decision. They must also keep proper records and accounts and deal properly with client's money and must make provision to be able to compensate you if you make a valid claim against them.

Complaining

The rules and regulations which now control investment business are supposed to be in the interests of the consumer. You should deal only with people who are members of FIMBRA, LAUTRO or one of the other self-regulating organizations. If you have a complaint, take it up first with the company. If that gets you nowhere, or the company has gone bust, complain to the regulating organization to which the company belonged.

In addition to these safeguards, there are now a growing number of private ombudsmen. These private ombudsmen are different from the public ones. First, they are specific to one kind of financial service and are ultimately paid for by the companies which they investigate. Their investigations are therefore limited to the companies who join and support the scheme – who are in any case generally the more responsible ones. Second, the companies generally agree to abide by the decisions of their ombudsman subject to a limit on their financial liability. Third, they investigate a broader range of complaints that go beyond maladministration. They can actually investigate the decisions made by the companies and not just the way they have carried out their policies.

So far there are three of these ombudsman services, though more will probably appear in 1988/89. In all cases they seem to be genuinely independent even though, ultimately, they are paid for by the companies they watch over.

The Insurance Ombudsman

The insurance ombudsman deals with complaints against insurance companies. More than seventy companies participate in the service, including most of the big names.

The insurance ombudsman can consider a complaint about the size of a settlement, about a delay in dealing with your claim, about a refusal of a claim, and about any unfair or bad treatment. You can go through the ombudsman even in cases where you could go to court. However, you must wait to take court action until the insurance ombudsman has determined your case.

The insurance ombudsman will consider a case only after you have tried and failed to reach an agreement on your complaint with the company concerned. Normally your first complaint should be to the branch and then to the head office. You must contact the insurance ombudsman within six months of the company finally refusing to settle your complaint.

If the insurance ombudsman finds in your favour and you accept the decision, the insurance company will abide by the decision to pay you the amount recommended up to £100,000, or up to £10,000 a year in health insurance cases. If you accept the offer, you give up the right to go to court. If you reject the offer, you are free to go to court or pursue the matter some other way.

The insurance ombudsman is at 31 Southampton Row, London WC1B 5HJ (tel: 01–242 8613). You can find out from this office which companies are members and can obtain a leaflet about the service.

The Banking Ombudsman

The banking ombudsman began work on 1 January 1986. All of the well-known high street banks are members of the scheme and about 98% of all bank customers are covered by it.

The banking ombudsman deals with complaints about all aspects of the normal business conducted by bank branches including bank accounts, cash machines and loans. But he cannot deal with complaints about the commercial judgement of the bank. So he cannot investigate whether the bank was right to refuse you an overdraft. He cannot investigate the way the bank has used its discretion under a will or trust. And he cannot investigate a matter that has gone to court. The matter must be for an amount of less than £50,000.

You must have tried to resolve the matter with the bank branch and the head office and you must complain to the ombudsman within six months of your last contact with the bank's head office.

If the banking ombudsman finds in your favour, the bank will accept the decision and pay the sum recommended up to £50,000. If you accept the decision, you cannot then go to court. But if you reject it, you can pursue the matter through the courts if you wish.

The banking ombudsman is at Citadel House, 5–11 Fetter Lane, London EC4A 1BR (tel: 01–583 1395).

The Building Societies Ombudsman

The building societies ombudsman investigates complaints about building societies. It is the newest of the services and there is less information about its activities. Almost all building societies are members. The only exceptions are a very few very small local ones.

The complaint must be about maladministration or unfair treatment or that the society has breached its legal or contractual obligations. And it must have caused you financial loss or inconvenience. The building societies ombudsman cannot investigate a decision on a person's creditworthiness but he can investigate maladministration in dealing with an assessment of creditworthiness. You cannot pursue a case through the ombudsman if it has been to court or is currently going through a court.

Before complaining to the ombudsman you should try to resolve the matter with the society and you must bring your complaint within a reasonable time to the ombudsman.

If the building societies ombudsman finds in your favour, the building society can be ordered to pay you up to £100,000. But the society can avoid this order by making a statement to its members as to why it is not accepting the decision. It must also make the reason for not paying you public in the way the building societies ombudsman specifies.

The building societies ombudsman is at Grosvenor Gardens House, 35–37 Grosvenor Gardens, London SW1X 7AW (tel: 01–931 0044).

10 INHERITANCE TAX

In the 1986 Budget the chancellor announced a new way of taxing inherited property. A new tax, inheritance tax, was born out of an old one, capital transfer tax. In subsequent Budgets the new tax was made less onerous. But it will still affect the estates of people with possessions, including their home, worth more than £110,000 when they die. The tax is also payable on gifts made within seven years of death. This chapter looks at inheritance tax and, briefly, at capital gains tax.

Tax on Estates

Large estates have been taxed since 1894. The estate duty introduced then remained substantially the same until replaced and extended by capital transfer tax in 1974. Estate duty was known as the voluntary tax. Wealthy people could avoid its provisions by transfers in and out of trusts, or simply by trying to give their assets to their heirs at least seven years before they died.

Capital transfer tax was intended to stop all that. Every gift or 'transfer' during a person's life was added up or 'cumulated'. Tax was payable as soon as the total of lifetime gifts exceeded a certain figure – £67,000 in 1985/86. Death was the final transfer and assets passing on death were added on to the total lifetime gifts and taxed in the same way, though at a higher rate. As the total gifts mounted, so the rate of tax increased until, at £300,000 or more, tax on death was levied at 60% in 1985/86. An even higher top rate of 75% on estates over £2.65 million existed until 1984.

Despite the draconian appearance of capital transfer tax, it brought in less money than estate duty. There were many exemptions. Transfers between spouses were entirely free of the tax. At least £3,000 could be given away in any year without coming into the arithmetic at all. And each Budget brought more reliefs. Some allowed forests to be passed on intact, others helped family businesses to be handed down. In recent years the rates of tax were substantially reduced and the income levels to which they applied raised. And from 1981 gifts were cumulated just over the last ten years rather than over the donor's whole lifetime. In effect, that meant that nearly £10,000 could be given away each year without fear of the tax.

Transition

As a result of all these changes, the lifetime gift part of capital transfer tax was bringing in only £55 million a year, about 6% of the total revenue of the tax. So in 1986 the chancellor decided to abolish this part of capital transfer tax altogether and leave just the tax to deal with estates passing on death. This amended tax is inheritance tax and it came into force on 18 March 1986. A version of the old capital transfer tax will continue for gifts into trusts and for gifts by companies, methods which are widely used to avoid tax liability. But otherwise any gift or legacy, including one made before 18 March 1986, is now dealt with under the new rules.

The New Tax

Inheritance tax is a tax on the value of property passing on death and within seven years of death. The tax is levied after death and is normally paid from the estate. But if you have given away enough money so that the cumulative seven-year total exceeds the current threshold for inheritance tax of £110,000, then, on your death, tax may well be due on a pre-death gift. If so, it is the recipient who must pay the tax due on it. Gifts made within three years of death attract the full rate of tax and those made between three and seven years of death are liable for a reduced rate of tax. That rule applies equally to gifts made before 18 March 1986.

Gifts which would be taxed if the donor died within seven years are called potentially exempt transfers. If the donor survives seven years, they become completely exempt. There is no obligation on the donor or the recipient to inform the Capital Taxes Office of any gift which is a potentially exempt transfer. But it would save the executors of your will a lot of trouble if you did keep a record.

On death, the tax due is calculated on the total amount of the assets passing on death added to all gifts made within seven years of death after the various exemptions listed below. In 1988/89 the tax starts when the total exceeds £110,000. This amount will normally go up each year.

Exemptions
As well as the £110,000 starting point, there are many ways of giving money away exempt from inheritance tax. All gifts made more than seven years before death are totally exempt. Within the seven years before death, you will be able to give away up to

£3,000 a year without it coming into the arithmetic at all. This £3,000 exemption can be carried forward by one year. So if you make no gifts in one year you can give up to £6,000 in the next (prior to 6 April 1981 this exemption was £2,000). In addition to this exemption you can also make gifts of up to £250 each to any number of individuals in each tax year, though they cannot also gain from the £3,000 exemption. You can give up to £2,500 to a grandchild on their wedding (or £5,000 to your own child, or £1,000 to anyone!). You can also make a gift of any size for the maintenance of a dependent relative. All these amounts will be completely ignored in the seven years before death. You can usually ignore half the value of a business which you own or control. However, any gifts outside these amounts will be added on to your estate and tax calculated accordingly. The exemptions apply to individuals, so a husband and wife can give away twice as much.

These exemptions apply only to gifts made before death. On death, different exemptions apply. Inheritance by a spouse is entirely free of the tax, though this does *not* mean that a couple should not worry about the tax (see 'Minimizing Inheritance Tax' on page 100). All legacies to a registered charity or to a political party with at least two MPs are free of inheritance tax (there are nine parties which come within the definition). There are also special exemptions for property, including buildings and works of art, which forms part of the national heritage.

Rate of Tax
Working out the tax due is quite straightforward in most cases unless you have given away so much money that the cumulative seven-year total exceeds £110,000 at any time within the last seven years. If

you have, you can probably afford to get private advice from a specialist solicitor or accountant, and I strongly advise you to do so!

In order to work out what level of inheritance tax your heirs would face if you died tomorrow, write down the gifts you have made in the last seven years. Remember to take away the exemptions set out above from each year's total gifts. Then add on the value of your house less any outstanding mortgage (if you do not own your house, there is far less likelihood of your having to pay inheritance tax) and any other assets which will pass to your heirs. Remember to include your furniture and effects within the house and any motor car you have. It does not matter how many people you share them among, the same tax will be due on the total.

If the total is below £110,000, you will not have to worry about inheritance tax. If it is above that amount, inheritance tax will be due. There is now one rate of 40%.

For example, Ruby Ellison has been giving her three children capital from her late husband's life insurance policy over the last few years. Five years ago she gave away £9,000, four years ago £7,995, three years ago £10,005, two years ago £7,005 and last year she gave another £7,005. If Ruby died tomorrow, she would leave a house, property and cash worth £150,000. Table 10 opposite summarizes these figures.

On her death the net estate of £173,010 would be taxed as follows:

	Tax due (£)
110,000 × 0% =	Nil
63,010 × 40% =	25,204

Table 10
Inheritance Tax 1988/89

	Years before death	Exemption available (£)	Gifts (£)	Exemption used (£)*	Net transfer (£)	Cumulative transfer (£)
1981/82	7	3,000	0	0	0	0
1982/83	6	3,000	0	0	0	0
1983/84	5	3,000	9,000	6,000	3,000	3,000
1984/85	4	3,000	7,995	3,000	4,995	7,995
1985/86	3	3,000	10,005	3,000	7,005	15,000
1986/87	2	3,000	7,005	3,000	4,005	19,005
1987/88	1	3,000	7,005	3,000	4,005	23,010
1988/89	0	3,000	150,000	nil	150,000	173,010
Total			191,010	18,000	173,010	

* An exemption not used one year can be carried forward to the next.

99

Ruby's case is relatively straightforward because the cumulative total of her gifts never exceeded the threshold for inheritance or capital transfer tax. In cases where it does, there are lower rates of tax on gifts made at least three years before death. The full rate of tax is reduced by 20% for each year from the third year, thus becoming zero for gifts made at least seven years before death.

Minimizing Inheritance Tax

Although inheritance tax is aimed at very large estates, many people, particularly in the south-east of England, now own a house which alone would be liable to the tax when they die.

If you think you may have more than £110,000 to leave when you die, especially if you have given away large amounts of money or valuables in the last few years, you should seek advice. There are schemes around which offer ways to reduce the impact of inheritance tax. But do take care before embarking on any plan which creates artificial arrangements to avoid inheritance tax. If you adopt a scheme which later is ruled to be invalid, it will be your heirs, not the person who sold it to you, who are liable for the tax.

If you are concerned, the simplest and safest thing you can do is to give away money or valuables to your heirs up to the value of the exemptions each year. If you want to make a larger gift, you should consider taking out a life insurance policy which would pay sufficient to cover the tax should you die within seven years. If you survive beyond seven years, the policy lapses.

However, there is not much you can do about the value of your house. There are special restrictions to stop you giving away a house and continuing to live in it. It is counted as yours until you stop having any benefit from it at all. So unless you give your home away outright and stop living in it at least seven years before you die, it will count as part of your estate. There is some softening of the rules in cases of medical or personal necessity. But normally the house you live in will have to pass intact, and if it is worth more than £110,000, then tax will be due.

A couple with a large estate which they own jointly should consider separating it so that they each own a part of it. They should then draw up new wills each leaving their part to their children or grandchildren. If they do not do that, the children will end up paying more tax when the second parent dies. For example, an estate worth £200,000 will attract no tax if the first of a couple to die leaves £100,000 to their children and the remainder to the survivor and no tax when the survivor dies and leaves the remaining £100,000 to the children. But if the first to die leaves the whole estate to the survivor who then dies and leaves the whole amount to the children, tax of £36,000 will be due on the total of £200,000.

Similarly, it is as well to skip a generation and pass on some property to grandchildren if leaving it to the children would then boost their own estate in later life.

However, these considerations are mainly for rich families. For most people the tax is due largely because their house is worth a lot of money and there is little that can be done to avoid paying that. And do remember in your keenness to avoid inheritance tax not to leave yourself without adequate resources in old age. Younger relatives may be very grateful for pre-death gifts, but they will not expect to use them to support you!

The inheritance tax rules are different in important respects from the capital transfer tax rules. If you have made a will intending to make the best of the capital transfer tax rules, consider changing it to take account of inheritance tax. If you have recently benefited from a will made before inheritance tax, you can alter the arrangements made in the will if you act within two years of the death. If these arrangements were made to minimize liability to capital transfer tax, others may now be more suitable. The arrangements can be altered to ensure that they minimize future obligations to inheritance tax. In order to change the terms of a will in this way, all the beneficiaries of the will have to agree. A new document, called a deed of family arrangement, is then signed by all parties. You should consult a solicitor if you think that you are in this position. But you have to act within two years of the death and inform the Capital Taxes Office within six months of making the deed.

There is a new official guide to inheritance tax available free from the nearest Capital Taxes Office (see the Appendix for addresses).

Capital Gains Tax

Capital gains tax is a tax on the increased value of an asset. You pay it when you sell the asset for a profit. Any gain realized on the sale of the house in which you live is exempt. Other gains are taxed at your rate of income tax if they exceed £5,000 in 1988/89. There is a complex system of revaluing assets to take account of inflation. Only the gain from March 1982 is counted.

Capital gains tax can be payable on the extra value of your own business when you sell it. But there is a special relief for people selling a business on retirement if they or their spouse have owned it for at least ten years. To benefit from this relief you have to be at least sixty. The age can be even lower if you are so ill that you cannot carry on with the business. In that case you will need medical evidence. The relief is total exemption from tax on the first £125,000 gain and half-exemption on the next £500,000 gain.

11   MAKING A WILL

Many people think that making a will is just for the rich. But more and more people own a house or have savings, and even your furniture and effects are likely to be worth well into five figures. This chapter explains how to ensure that the right people get it. It does not, however, cover the law in Scotland, which is different.

There is nothing morbid about making a will. On the contrary, it is a recognition that everyone is mortal and that you want your relatives and loved ones to find your affairs in an orderly and responsible state when you do die. If you do not make a will, your relatives will have a more difficult job and the property will be divided according to strict legal rules rather than to your wishes.

You can draw up a will yourself or you can use a solicitor. It is certainly safer to use a legally qualified advisor, although even solicitors can make errors. But if you are reasonably confident of your own abilities and your affairs are straightforward, there is no reason why you should not draw up a will yourself. If you want to do so it is essential that you get one of the many books which explain the procedure in full, such as *Wills and Probate*, edited by Edith Rudinger and published by the Consumers Association.

Even if you use a solicitor, there are many steps you can take before you see him or her which will reduce the time the job takes the solicitor and thus keep your charges low. You should expect to pay £50 to £100 for a straightforward will.

Executors

You have to decide who to name in the will as your executor(s). They will do all the work of winding up your affairs after your death. They have to collect all your property, including getting valuations and realizing the value of investments, pay all debts and taxes, deal with funeral and administration costs and then distribute the balance of your estate according to the terms of the will.

Being an executor is a detailed and time-consuming job. Normally the will provides for a payment to the executors for the work: £300 is reasonable for a non-professional but a professional will want to be allowed to charge his or her full fee. If the executors are relatives and also beneficiaries, this payment may be less or nominal. If the executor is not a beneficiary, it may be a friend or someone completely impartial who does the job for a professional fee – a solicitor or a bank, for example. The latter can be very expensive, and if there is a beneficiary who can take on the task it will be in their interest if you name them as executor. You can appoint more than one executor: that can help share the burden. There is a problem, however, if you appoint one relative and one professional. Both have duties and rights and you can find that the professional insists on doing the work and charging the fee. The will must provide for the fee for a professional or for a specific gift to someone who does the job as a friend or relative.

What You Own

The next step is to write down what you own with approximate values. You may be surprised at what it amounts to. You can get an estimate of the value of your personal possessions from the insurance policy for your house contents. Make sure that you include the value of any life insurance policies and, of course, the value of your home after any mortgage has been redeemed. If you are married, remember that much of your property is jointly owned and that only half the value is yours.

Who Inherits?

Normally it is a straightforward matter to decide who inherits your property. You make a few special dispositions of small items to named people – grandchildren, perhaps, or friends – and then leave the balance of your estate to your husband or wife or, if they are dead or die before you, to your children.

But life is not always that simple. You may have married more than once, have no living children, or have particular feelings about relatives who are already well off or who have always been closer to you. And there may be inheritance tax considerations (see Chapter 10).

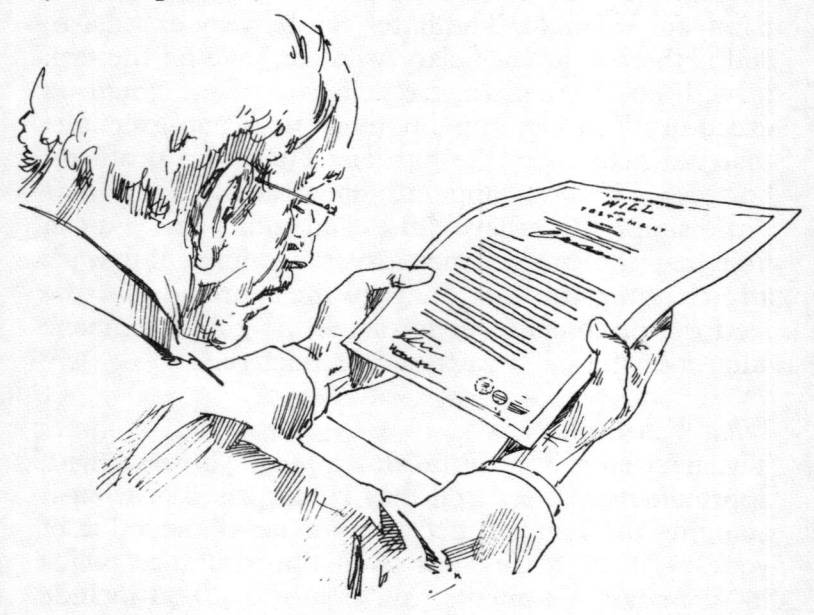

However, there are some people whom you can no longer totally disinherit. A husband or wife, an unmarried former spouse, a child, including an illegitimate child or one who is an adopted or *de facto* child, or anyone whom you maintained immediately prior to death can all apply to the court after your death if the will does not make reasonable financial provision for them. The court can then change the will to make such provision.

Remember too that those who survive you will have to live with any inequalities or perceived unfairness in the will.

After you have decided on any specific amounts of money or items of property that you wish to give to specific individuals, the balance or residue of your estate will normally pass to one person or to more than one person in equal (or sometimes unequal) shares.

In some cases, the main beneficiary in a will dies at the same time as or before you. A husband and wife may be killed together in an accident, for example. So it is sensible to include provision in the will for such an eventuality. If a husband and wife simply make wills leaving everything to the other, a joint death will leave them as if they had made no will at all. The rules which apply in such cases are complex and are explained below.

If the beneficiary is your son or daughter and they die first, any child or grandchild of theirs will inherit instead. In other cases, anything left to a beneficiary who dies before you simply goes into the residue of your estate. The beneficiary's relatives cannot inherit on their behalf.

Changing a Will
Your will comes into effect only on your death. So

you can change it at any time by making another or by amending it. However, if you marry, any will you made before the marriage is normally void. If you do not make a new one, your estate is divided up as if you had made no will. This provision can particularly affect widows or widowers who remarry. If they make no new will, the new husband or wife will inherit all their possessions and probably most of their money under the intestacy rules, which are described below. So if you want to ensure that your friends or even your children do get your share of things, you should make a new will once you are married. (See Chapters 5 and 6 for information on tax and widows. Information about social security for widows can be found in Chapter 4 of *Saga Rights Guide*, also by Paul Lewis in this series.)

Your heirs can also have the terms of your will re-arranged if some other arrangement would be to the advantage of all of them, for example to minimize inheritance tax (see Chapter 10) or to keep a property intact. To do that they must act within two years of the death and all the beneficiaries of the will have to agree. A new document, called a deed of family arrangement, is then signed by all parties. A family who wants to make such a deed should definitely consult a solicitor.

If You Die Without a Will

If you die without making a valid will, you are said to die 'intestate' and the law lays down rules of intestacy to determine who should inherit your property. The rules are complicated.

First, there is no executor because you have left no instructions in your will. Instead, there is an administrator. The nearest relative has the right to apply to be the administrator – normally it is the spouse or child of the deceased. Administrators have similar duties to executors.

If there is a surviving spouse and surviving children or grandchildren, the spouse inherits all personal possessions, including furniture, motor cars and jewellery and the first £40,000 of the rest. The surviving spouse also retains a life interest in half of the balance of the estate. The other half is divided among the children (or, if they are dead, the grandchildren) who also inherit the first half on the death of the remaining spouse.

Similar rules apply if there is a surviving spouse and a surviving parent or sibling of the deceased except that the spouse gets £85,000 and half the remainder instead of £40,000 and a life interest in half the remainder. If there are no children, parents or siblings, the spouse inherits the whole estate.

If there is no surviving spouse, any children (or grandchildren) inherit in equal shares. If there are no children (or grandchildren), the parents of the deceased inherit. If they are dead, the inheritance passes on through relatives in a strict order of precedence starting with any brothers or sisters of the deceased, then their children, and so on into more remote degrees of relationship. But only blood relatives can be considered as beneficiaries. If no one is entitled, the estate passes to the Crown.

So do not die without making a will!

USEFUL ADDRESSES

There are many useful addresses and sources of help scattered throughout the text. This appendix lists some other useful sources of advice and information.

For many problems the first place to go is your local **Citizens Advice Bureau**. There are over 1,000 CAB offices throughout the UK so most people are within easy reach of one. If they cannot help you with the problem themselves, they will know who can help locally and where to go. They are in the phone book under 'Citizens Advice Bureau' and your local library or post office should have their address as well. Many of them operate restricted opening hours, so it is a good idea to phone first before travelling any distance to visit them.

Age Concern has local offices throughout Britain. Some will be able to give advice, especially on local services. You will normally find the local group under 'Age Concern' in the phone book, but sometimes they are still under their old title 'Old People's Welfare Council'. **Age Concern England** is at 60 Pitcairn Road, Mitcham, Surrey CR4 3LL (tel: 01–640 5431). **Age Concern Scotland** is at 33 Castle Street, Edinburgh EH2 3DN (tel: 031–225 5000). **Age Concern Wales** is at 4th Floor, 1 Cathedral Road, Cardiff CF1 9SD (tel: 0222 371821). **Age Concern Northern Ireland** is at 6 Lower Crescent, Belfast BT7 1NR (tel: 0232 235729).

Help the Aged produce advice sheets and useful publications which you can find out about from their head office at St James's Walk, London EC1R 0BE (tel: 01–253 0253).

If you want general information about social security, you can telephone **Freeline Social Security**. This information service is run by the DHSS but is completely independent of the local offices. They can advise you about social security rules and benefits and are generally very good. They cannot advise you about your own particular case. Their number is 0800 666 555. The call is free.

Your local **social security office** should carry a full range of leaflets about social security benefits, including the very useful *Which Benefit?* (number FB.2) which lists all the other leaflets they produce, and *Social Security Benefit Rates* (number NI.196) which lists all the benefit rates. FB.2 is also available from post offices. If you cannot get a DHSS leaflet from any other source, contact the DHSS Leaflets Unit at PO Box 21, Stanmore, Middlesex HA7 1AY.

The **Company Pensions Information Centre** publish some useful leaflets and will give you general advice about how company pensions work. They are at 7 Old Park Lane, London W1Y 3LJ (tel: 01–493 4757). The **Occupational Pensions Advisory Service** will advise you on any problems with your own pension scheme once you have retired. Contact them through your local CAB or at Aviation House, 129 Kingsway, London WC2 6NN (tel: 01–379 7311).

The **Pre-Retirement Association** offers help, advice and courses to people approaching or just reaching retirement and can help you find part-time work once you have retired. They charge a membership fee of £16 a year. Contact them at 19 Undine Street, London SW17 8PP.

You can get advice about making money from your home from **Age Concern England** at 60 Pitcairn

Road, Mitcham, Surrey CR4 3LL (tel: 01–640 5431). They publish two useful booklets, *Housing Options for Older People* and *Using Your Home as Capital* (price £1.95 each).

There are many books on income tax but few of them are aimed at older people. Look at them carefully before buying. The Inland Revenue publish some useful leaflets, including *Income Tax and Pensioners* (number IR4), *Income Tax Age Allowance* (number IR4A) and *Income Tax and Widows* (number IR23). There are many others covering such things as separation, divorce, death, appealing, foreign pensions, and so on. You can obtain them from your local tax office: look this up in the phone book under 'Inland Revenue'.

A quick glance in a newsagent will show you the extraordinary range of investment magazines that now exist. And there are books as well on every kind of investment. Many of them are not good value for money. Check them carefully before purchase.

The **British Insurance Brokers' Association** will put you in touch with a local insurance broker and offers an arbitration service if you have a complaint. They also produce some useful leaflets. They are at BIBA House, 14 Bevis Marks, London EC3A 7NT (tel: 01–623 9043).

The **Securities and Investments Board (SIB)** regulates the bodies which regulate financial advisors. They are at 3 Royal Exchange Buildings, London EC3V 3NL. Two of the bodies they regulate are the **Financial Intermediaries, Managers and Brokers Regulatory Association (FIMBRA)** at 22 Great Tower Street, London EC3R 5AQ (tel: 01–929 2711) and the **Life Assurance and Unit Trust Regulatory Organization (LAUTRO)** at Centre Point, 103 New Oxford Street, London WC1A 1QH (tel: 01–379

0444). They all produce some explanatory leaflets and you should contact them in cases of query or complaint about financial advisors.

There are several commercial books about inheritance tax and some free ones from companies promoting particular schemes which claim to minimize it. The official guide is called *Inheritance Tax* and is free from the **Capital Taxes Office** at Minford House, Rockley Road, London E14 0DF (tel: 01–603 4622).

Post offices have a limited range of leaflets about social security, including FB.6, *Retiring*, which contains very general information. All post offices carry leaflets about the National Savings products and Government stock. Many post offices, especially smaller ones, can also give you useful local addresses.

Saga Holidays is at The Saga Building, Middelburg Square, Folkestone, Kent CT20 1AZ (tel: 0303 40000). They offer holidays and other services for the over-sixties and publish a monthly, *Saga Magazine*, which is available on subscription only.

The **Consumers Association** publishes a lot of useful books and a monthly magazine called *Which?*. It is at 14 Buckingham Street, London WC2N 6DS (tel: 01–839 1222).

Finally, there are other addresses especially to do with disability and social security in *Saga Rights Guide*, also by Paul Lewis in this series.

saga
FOOD GUIDE

Retirement is an excellent time to take more pleasure in cooking and enjoying your food – and a time to improve your diet to keep in good shape. This book is full of advice and inspiration on subjects such as:

- Basic nutrition ● Cooking for one or two
- Tips for beginners ● Entertaining
- Good value meals ● Convenience foods
- Catering for grandchildren ● Picnics
- Clever shopping

Each section ends with two or three recipes, and the book includes advice on specialist diets, vegetarianism, fats and fibres.

Carol Leverkus is a freelance nutritionist with a special interest in healthy diets for the retirement age group.

Other books in this series

Saga Rights Guide
Saga Health Guide
Saga Leisure Guide
Saga Property Guide

saga
RIGHTS GUIDE

This guide clearly outlines the many rights, concessions and services which become available to you on your retirement.

- Pensions, both within the UK and abroad
- Illness and disability provisions
- Help with a low income • Rate and rent rebates
- Legal aid • Motor insurance

These are just some of the issues clarified in this book. Concluding with useful addresses, and information about complaints procedures and ombudsmen, this is an essential reference book to steer you through today's complex bureaucracy.

Paul Lewis is a freelance writer who contributes regularly to *Saga Magazine*, and is an expert on financial and legal matters.

Other books in this series

Saga Property Guide
Saga Health Guide
Saga Food Guide
Saga Leisure Guide

saga
LEISURE GUIDE

Your retirement is the opportunity to do all those things you've hoped to do but never had the time.

- Long distance luxury cruises
- Weekend breaks ● Caravanning
- University courses ● Charity work
- New sports and pastimes

These are just some of the many ideas explored in this book. The *Saga Leisure Guide* includes a questionnaire on your qualities as a retiree and offers advice on courses to prepare you for this new phase. This is the book to ensure that your retirement is the time of your life.

Roy Johnstone is a freelance journalist and a regular contributor to *Saga Magazine* on leisure issues.

Other books in this series

Saga Property Guide
Saga Health Guide
Saga Food Guide
Saga Rights Guide

saga
HEALTH GUIDE

The SAGA HEALTH GUIDE offers explanation and down to earth advice on how to keep in the best possible physical shape during your retirement. It covers all the most common questions and worries that arise, such as:

- Body changes • Exercises for fitness
- Aches and pains • Looking after your heart
- Stress • Sleeping well
- Common medical problems
- Women's health

In addition it includes suggestions on diets and hints for overcoming sight and hearing difficulties.

Dr Muir Gray specialises in the health problems of people of advancing years, and works at the John Radcliffe Infirmary in Oxford.

Other books in this series

Saga Food Guide
Saga Property Guide
Saga Rights Guide
Saga Leisure Guide

saga
PROPERTY GUIDE

Retirement is a time when many of us reassess our housing requirements, and start to look to the future. This book gives practical common sense advice on all the concerns that most often arise, including:

- The pros and cons of moving to a smaller home
- Holiday resorts • Sheltered Housing
- Living abroad • Nursing homes
- Buying and selling property
- Legal and financial aspects

Concluding with lists of addresses of builders, trade and aid organizations specializing in retirement housing, this invaluable guide will equip you to take the housing decisions best suited to your needs.

Michael Dineen is a regular Saga contributor and writes a weekly property column for *The Observer*.

Other books in this series

Saga Rights Guide
Saga Leisure Guide
Saga Food Guide
Saga Health Guide